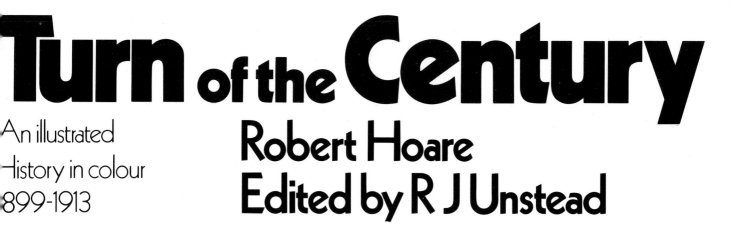

Turn of the Century

An illustrated
History in colour
1899-1913

Robert Hoare
Edited by R J Unstead

Special Adviser:
Dr J M Roberts
Fellow and Tutor in Modern History
at Merton College, Oxford

Macdonald Educational

Turn of the Century

Contents

A MACDONALD BOOK

© Macdonald Educational Ltd 1975

First published in Great Britain in 1975
Reprinted 1979, 1983, 1985

All rights reserved

SBN 0 356 05088 2

Printed and bound in Great Britain by
Purnell and Sons (Book Production) Ltd
Paulton, Bristol

Published by
Macdonald & Company (Publishers) Ltd
Maxwell House
74 Worship Street
London EC2A 2EN

Members of BPCC plc

◀ **A fashionable "New Woman".** Women were starting to play a new part in society.

The poor in Russia. Despite great social advances, poverty was still widespread.

At the turn of the century, as at the turn of a year, people looked forward to a better tomorrow, and for many there was reason for hope. Some of the worst effects of the Industrial Revolution had been lessened by an increased social awareness of governments and militancy of workers.

A wide range of inventions was now having its effect. Electric lighting had arrived, though gas was far more common. The telephone was in use in the major cities of the industrialized world and, in offices, secretaries were already clattering away on typewriters. Motor cars were becoming more common on the roads and, in 1909, Blériot awakened Europe to the significance of aviation by flying across the English Channel.

Daring experiments were being made in the arts. Sport was being enjoyed by more people and popular newspapers and magazines were bringing ordinary people glimpses of worlds beyond their everyday lives. By 1913, cinema was delighting mass audiences.

There had been no war in Europe since 1871. Yet, despite the optimism of the age, a succession of clashes in Africa, in the Near and Far East contributed to an atmosphere of international tension. Could a great war between the major powers be averted?

Western Society

"In this land of abounding wealth, probably more than a fourth of the population are living in poverty."

These words were written in 1901 by Seebohm Rowntree, the British social reformer. Britain had been the first country to achieve industrialization, but by 1900, the social problems that Britain faced were largely shared by all advanced countries, including those of Western Europe and the United States.

In Britain's fast-growing towns, for example, the workers were crowded together in slum conditions. For the poorest, life was a grim struggle. They found refuge in drink, and Saturday nights in the towns were disturbed by drunkenness and rioting.

Yet the lot of the poor was better than their predecessors' had been, half a century earlier. People were more concerned about public health. Housing and sanitation were receiving closer attention, and the risk of epidemics of diseases like cholera had been considerably reduced.

As time went by, some of the better-off workers were able to move out of the teeming city centres to new homes in the suburbs. These were still built in terraced rows, but now they often had small gardens. By 1913, many people were travelling to work from the suburbs in the new motor buses.

Yet the gulf between the rich and the great mass of the poor was still enormous. With taxation low and servants cheap, the rich were able to lead lives of leisured opulence. They maintained country estates and elegant town residences, enjoyed balls, house-parties, sport, theatre and foreign travel. The mass of the poor, by contrast, engaged in a ceaseless struggle against insecurity and want.

The years before World War One saw the development of much that was new in society—mass production, cinema, motoring, aviation and certain measures of social reform. It also saw the final flowering of a Golden Age for the rich. Their lives were never to be so secure and privileged again.

▲ **French soldier at the turn of the century.** In France, as in Germany, every able-bodied man had an obligation to serve in the forces, and both countries retained large armies.

Yet, from the end of the Franco-Prussian War in 1871, to 1900, there had been peace in Europe for nearly thirty years.

▶ **British road-menders in their lunch hour.** Life for the working man, woman and child was still very hard. However, in Britain, the Liberal government of 1906 introduced radical measures to protect the working classes. These included old age pensions, sickness and unemployment benefits. For the rich, income tax rose from one shilling to 1s. 2d. in the £.

A poor farm family in Kentucky. Small farmers could not compete with large-scale farming which used the latest agricultural machines. Cheap food benefited industrial workers but it created poverty for many farm workers. British farming was acutely depressed at this time.

▲ **A lower middle-class family at tea in Britain.** All classes benefited to some extent from the Empire. The tea this family is drinking probably came from one of Britain's colonies—India, Ceylon or Assan. Cheap tea, cocoa, sugar and coffee were small luxuries that even those with modest incomes could afford. People could now buy refrigerated meat, shipped from New Zealand and Australia.

▲ **A wealthy woman and child in the United States are pushed out for a ride by a Negro servant in livery.** Such women had no work to do, apart from supervising the household, since all the domestic tasks were carried out by a small army of servants.

◄ **Night scene in a pleasure park in Vienna.** Music and gaiety abounded for the wealthy, and even for the poor by comparison with any earlier age. Food and entertainment were cheap. Yet, beyond the bright lights, neglected children still slept in shop doorways.

5

France: the Golden Years

The Third French Republic was established in 1871. Under successive governments, France became richer and stronger.

She was still largely a land of peasants, but most owned their own farms and were prospering. Industry and commerce were expanding (though not as fast as in Germany). France was soon able to make large loans to other countries, and became known as the "Banker of Europe". She had also added to her possessions in Africa and South East Asia. By 1913, she had the second largest empire in the world.

Yet not all Frenchmen were content with the Republic. It had been set up after France's defeat by Prussia (1871) and most Frenchmen still thirsted for revenge. The powerful Catholic Church favoured a monarchy; the republicans in turn tried to weaken the hold of the Church. Division between the two came to a head over the Dreyfus case.

Dreyfus was a Jew, and many claimed that Jews were running the country and betraying it to Germany. The Republic, they claimed, could no longer guarantee France's security; a stronger form of government was needed. Catholics tended to side with these critics.

Republicans saw the case as an example of Catholics and monarchists in the army persecuting an innocent man. The affair split France, setting lifelong friends against each other. Yet the Republic survived. Known monarchists in the army were dismissed and a series of new laws attacked the privileges of the Catholic Church.

Many French socialists, however, felt that it was not enough to attack the privileges of the Church while the privileges of the rich were left largely intact. For all the splendour of fashionable Paris, the conditions of industrial workers often remained appalling. The great socialist leader, Jean Jaurès, persuaded some that improvements could be forced through peacefully. Others demanded the violent overthrow of the Republic. Strikes, riots and workers' demonstrations were rife in France's "Golden Years".

▲ **The elegant rich at Trouville,** a popular resort on the north coast of France. For the rich, this was the *Belle Époque* (beautiful era). Yet many felt threatened by radicals and Socialists in the Third Republic and wanted the return of a monarchy in France.

▲ **Poster of Sarah Bernhardt,** one of the greatest actresses of all time. Fashionable Parisians flocked to see her perform.

▲ **British cartoon of the** *Entente Cordiale* (friendly understanding) of 1904. This was a declaration by France and Britain of their agreement on certain issues of mutual interest. The *Entente* was not a firm alliance, but it was enough to make Germany nervous.

▲ **People of fashion at a** *salon* where works of art are on display. At the turn of the century, Paris was the centre of the artistic world. Among others, the young Picasso lived there.

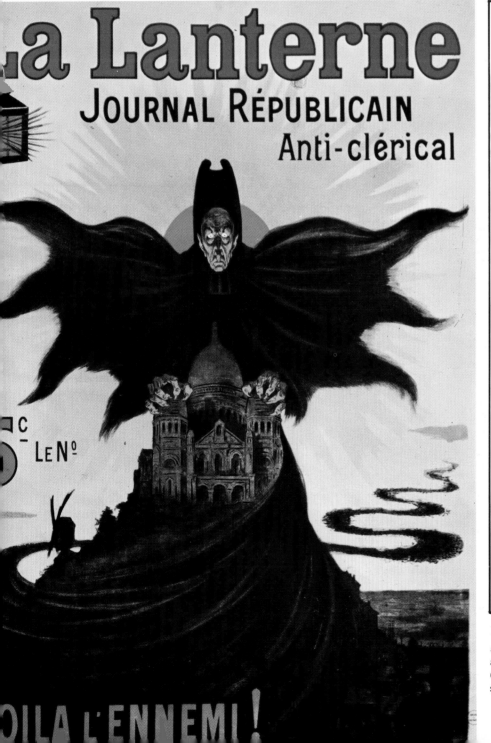

La Lanterne
JOURNAL RÉPUBLICAIN
Anti-clérical

VOILA L'ENNEMI!

▲ **Captain Alfred Dreyfus** (centre), a Jewish officer in the French army, was found guilty in 1894 of spying for Germany and imprisoned on Devil's Island for life.

Later indications of his innocence were found, but the army refused to re-try him. What followed is called the Dreyfus Affair, a great public argument over the rights and wrongs of the case. Many important people spoke out for Dreyfus, including the great novelist Emile Zola. At last, Dreyfus was tried again in 1899; but again found guilty. This time he was sentenced to 10 years, but the President pardoned him a few days later.

The Affair went on until, in 1906, the highest court in the land said that Dreyfus was innocent. He returned to the army and became a Brigadier-general.

◀ **This magazine,** *La Lanterne,* **was devoted to attacks on the Catholic Church.** Its cover shows a priest in the form of a vulture on the *Sacré Coeur,* a church that Republicans saw as a symbol of Catholic power.

Fashion

▲ Mrs Bloomer's ladies "trousers" for easy movement caused an outcry in the 1850s; **by 1900 leisure wear was established.**

▲ **This German advertisement for cigarettes** reveals a new freedom to display the female form. Moreover, it shows the women actually smoking, still considered very improper.

▶ **The Mayor of Vienna rides through a park in 1897.** The picture throws a spotlight on the fashions of the day.

Notice that all the men have top hats and most are wearing frock coats. Most also wear side-whiskers and moustaches or full beards. All the ladies have large hats, some have put up their parasols. It is a summer's day and they are wearing light dresses, perhaps of silk or satin, fastened modestly high at the neck. Some of the children are wearing straw boaters, later to be worn by men.

"We were forever changing our clothes," said Lady Cynthia Asquith about fashionable life at the turn of the century.

Different clothes were considered necessary for different occasions, and rich people of fashion always strove to be correctly dressed. At a house party on a winter Sunday, for example, a woman might wear a "best dress" of velvet for breakfast and church-going, and change afterwards into a tweed coat and skirt. In the late afternoon she might wear a tea-gown, and, for the evening meal, a dinner-gown.

Men also changed their clothes three or four times, choosing between formal dress, lounge suits and dinner suits, and wearing a sporting jacket with jodhpurs or knickerbockers if there was riding or walking. Formal dress consisted of a black frock coat and striped or check trousers, with a top hat, stick and gloves. Out of doors, a lady always wore a large, highly decorated hat. She might also wear a feather boa, or carry a parasol.

Skirts were long by today's standards, but they did sometimes reveal the wearer's ankles. The sheath dress, introduced in 1909, did not catch on, but a year later women began wearing hobble-skirts. These were very tight and often had a slit in the side.

▲ "Oh those Edwardian women! All they had to do was to wear the most expensive gowns, look delightfully bored and majestically useless." These are the words of a man who knew women like these. They are making last-minute preparations for a ball. Notice the young lady's shape—attained with the help of her maid and a tightly-laced corset. The hair-do's will have taken hours to arrange.

▲ The girl on the left is displaying the elegant underwear of her day including the formidable **whalebone corset.** The girl on the right is wearing an **Edwardian bathing-suit**—bold by Victorian standards.

▼ **The sheath skirt** caused a stir, as women lifted it up for free movement, showing "far more of the lower limbs than is desirable".

Suffragettes

"The argument of the broken window pane is the most valuable in modern politics." This was the belief of Mrs Emmeline Pankhurst, leader of the suffragettes in Britain.

The suffragettes were a group of women who wanted women to be allowed to vote in national elections. They not only smashed windows but also set fire to houses and railway stations, damaged valuable paintings and chained themselves to railings in public places.

The movement for the vote (suffrage) reflected deep changes that were taking place in women's position in society. They now worked, not only in industry, but as clerks, typists, and as telephonists. In Britain in 1900, there were already over 200 women doctors and over 100 women dentists. By 1910, women could become chartered accountants. How was it that women were allowed such responsibilities, yet not the vote?

As time passed, some middle-class women began to demand the vote with greater determination. In Britain, the Women's Social and Political Union was formed in 1903. At first, the W.S.P.U. relied on peaceful persuasion. Later they began to interrupt political meetings and even Parliament. Later still they became more violent. When they were arrested, some refused to eat, and often became so ill they had to be fed by force or else set free. Police behaviour towards the suffragettes was often rough and sometimes brutal.

Suffragettes in the United States were less militant than in England. Yet, by 1913, several states there had given women the vote. Women in Britain were still unable to vote in national elections at the outbreak of World War One. Indeed, women were allowed to vote in only one country in Europe—lone liberal Norway, where they had exercised the right since 1907.

▲ A typical scene of the times, this one taking place in France. **A suffragette is led away by an escort of gendarmes.**

▲ **Postcard making fun of suffragettes.** At first they were not taken seriously. Every music-hall comedian was certain of a laugh if he mentioned the word "suffragette". Later, annoyed by interruptions during a play or concert, men often violently attacked suffragettes.

▶ **Executive committee of the International Council for Women meeting in July 1899.** Second from the left in the front row is Susan Brownell Anthony, leader of the suffragettes in America. Activity in Britain inspired a revival of the women's movement there and Mrs Pankhurst visited America in 1912.

◀ **Derby Day in Britain, 1913.** As the field in the Derby thundered around Tattenham Corner, a figure ran out from the crowd and flung herself at King George V's horse, *Anmer*. She was a suffragette named Emily Davison. She was knocked to the ground, terribly injured, and died shortly afterwards. "A mad sacrifice", said many. But this dramatic act won a great deal of publicity for the suffragettes and the funeral was an immense procession in support of votes for women. The movement had a martyr to remember.

▼ **Cartoon attacks the so-called "Cat and Mouse Act" (1913) in Britain.** By this Act, a suffragette, once arrested, could be re-arrested at any time after her release. This meant that suffragettes who refused to eat could be released half dead from starvation and sent back to prison when they started taking an active part in the movement again.

By this time, suffragette disorder had reached its peak, and so had the reaction to it. Gangs of hooligans were breaking up women's meetings in the most violent way.

Science and Daily Life

No previous century had produced as many inventions as the 19th century.

Development took time, but, by the turn of the century, many inventions like those shown here had begun to transform society. Lighting, for example, was very much improved. The invention of the gas mantle in Austria-Hungary in 1885 provided a steady white light, suitable for close work, instead of a flickering flame.

For some people, the electric light was now available. It had been developed by Joseph Swan in England and Thomas Edison in the United States, and, in 1882, Edison installed electric lighting in part of New York.

Electricity was coming to challenge steam as a source of power for factories, and was also being used for driving vehicles. Electric trains, picking up power from a live rail beside the track, were introduced. In town, electric tramcars worked on a similar principle, running on tracks but picking up their

power from overhead lines by means of a long pole or trolley.

Telephones were coming into wider use. By 1900, one in every 50 people in the United States had a telephone. Marconi had invented "wireless" telegraphy which was now being widely used for communication at sea. Until 1907, however, it could only be used to transmit Morse code. Then, Lee de Forest, an American, invented a valve that made radio speech possible.

In the field of entertainment, Edison had produced the gramophone and the Lumière brothers the cinema. Less sensational inventions nevertheless had a significant effect on the pattern of life. They included the mechanical carpet sweeper, now mass produced, and sold at ten shillings (50p) each, and Mr Gillette's safety razor, which became popular in 1904. In that year, 12 million razor blades were sold.

▲ **Hammond typewriter of about 1900.** The first practical typewriter was produced in the United States by Christopher Latham Sholes, and, in 1873, the Remington Fire Arms Co. agreed to manufacture it. The first machines cost £21, yet there was no rush to buy them at this time.

However, by the turn of the century, the typewriter had become a recognized feature of office life.

▲ **A woman telephonist at the Manchester exchange in England, circa 1900.** The telephone, like the typewriter, had great social impact. It provided new opportunities of employment for women.

▲ **Two cameras of about 1900.** Left: leather-covered Frena No. 0 de luxe camera containing 40 flat films, with close-up lens in accompanying box. Right: Kodak No. 1, the first film-loaded box camera for the non-expert. Photography started in the 1840's with the use of glass plates. It was transformed in 1884 by George Eastman of the United States who invented flexible roll film. He later designed the Kodak camera which made photography a popular hobby.

▲ **Guglielmo Marconi.** Ignored in his native Italy, Marconi developed radio telegraphy in Britain. In 1901 he created a sensation by sending a "wire-less" signal across the Atlantic Ocean. By 1905, the major navies of the world were equipped with radio.

In 1910, the notorious British murderer Dr Crippen was escaping to Canada by ship; the captain alerted Scotland Yard by radio and Crippen was arrested on arrival.

▲ **Thomas Alva Edison,** who had a genius for inventing, developing and commercially marketing electrical appliances. Having developed the electric light, he improved Bell's telephone by adding a carbon microphone. He invented the gramophone in 1877 and at once patented it. During the late 1890's and early 1900's Edison was involved in the motion-picture field.

▲ **The electric tramcar comes to Portsmouth.** These men are working on an overhead support for the power line.

▲ **1913 performance of** *Made for Laughs,* **starring the Keystone Cops.** On 28 December 1895, in the Grand Café on the Boulevard des Capucines in Paris, a startled crowd watched moving pictures of a train entering a station, a rowing boat leaving harbour and workers coming out of a factory. It was the world's first cinema show, put on by two brothers, Louis and Auguste Lumière.

But although the "cinematograph" or projector was invented in France, it was in the United States that the motion picture industry really became established. Films were, of course, still silent.

◄ **Bicycle advertisement of the turn of the century.** The first bicycle with wheels of matching sizes driven by a chain was manufactured by the Englishman James Starley in 1885. It was known as the "safety" bicycle. Three years later, John Boyd Dunlop, a Scottish vet living in Belfast, invented the pneumatic tyre which made cycling on the bumpy roads of the period easier. After this, cycling for leisure became highly popular with women as well as men.

13

Early Motoring

The motor car has led to notable changes in social habits in the modern world. But, at the turn of the century, the usefulness of the motor car had not yet been fully realized.

In 1902, an English motoring magazine *Motors and Motoring* said, "Motoring is a sport". At this time, motor cars were still thought of as horseless carriages—open ones at that.

To travel in a car was to suffer bumping on inadequate roads, to be enveloped in a choking cloud of dust in the summer and to suffer the permanent risk of a breakdown. Early pneumatic tyres were not very sturdy, and punctures were frequent.

The first cars frightened the horse traffic on the roads and the cattle in the fields, killed hens and sometimes knocked down pedestrians. Their passage was often followed by shouts of anger and furiously waved fists. But the motor car soon became something that the rich must possess.

The first petrol-driven car for sale to the public was produced in Germany in 1886 by Karl Benz. It was a three-wheeler able to travel at 10 m.p.h. By 1900, however, the four-wheeled car had long been usual.

Cars were extremely expensive, for they had to be built one at a time. In England, to cater for the demands of the rich, Henry Royce and the Hon. C. S. Rolls built a world-famous car, the *Silver Ghost*. It was not until 1908 that Henry Ford brought on to the market the world's first mass-produced car in the United States. His Model T Ford brought down the price and placed motoring within the reach of a great many more people.

Thereafter, as the number of cars grew, road surfaces had to be improved. They were coated with liquid tar to reduce dust. By 1913, there were some 66,000 licensed vehicles in the United States, about a third of this number in Britain and about a sixth in some other European countries.

▲ **An early motor bus.** They took over from horse-buses in the early 1900's. By 1910, there were over 6,000 motor cabs plying for hire in London. The last horse bus ran from Moorgate to London Bridge in 1911.

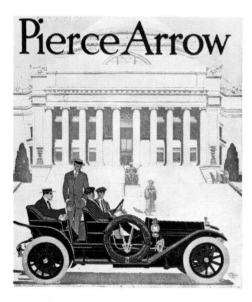

▲ **American advertisement for a luxury car.** At first, the car was very much a rich man's plaything—what would now be called a status symbol—evidence of wealth and power.

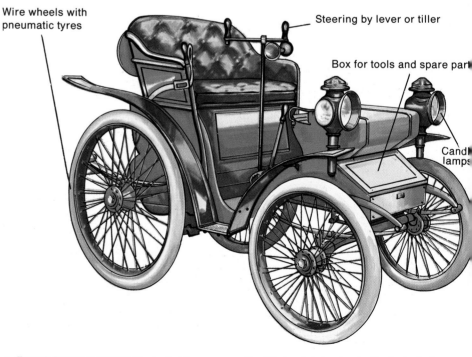

Wire wheels with pneumatic tyres

Steering by lever or tiller

Box for tools and spare parts

Candle lamps

▲ **French Peugeot of 1896.** Typical of the cars of its time, it has the shape of a light, horse-drawn carriage. The engine was placed under the seat. On the bumpy roads, keeping hold of the tiller was not easy, particularly during a gear-change. The brakes on this type of car were also very uncertain and driving it was really rather dangerous.

▲ **Two examples of fanciful headgear for fashionable female motorists.** More common headgear for women was a flat hat with a voluminous veil which covered the whole of the wearer's head and fastened at the neck. It was worn with a long dust-coat. Men wore peaked caps and large goggles. In winter, mufflers and heavy gloves were needed. Women often took knitting with them—to pass the time during breakdowns!

◄ **An early motor car raises a stir in a country village.** In Britain, as late as 1910, women sent a petition to the Queen asking for "relief from motor cars". "Our children are always in danger and our things are ruined by dust," they said. Some countries did have speed limits (in Britain it was 20 m.p.h. in 1903) but they were often exceeded by drivers using a variety of tricks to deceive the police.

The luxurious *Graf und Stift* **car in which the**
-fated Archduke Franz Ferdinand was to ride
his death in 1914. By then, every royal family
Europe had a car, and some members, like
ritain's King Edward VII (died 1910) were
nthusiastic motorists.

Mass Society

"Mass society" means a society in which differences between social classes have largely disappeared and people's needs and tastes are taken to be alike.

▲ **Body is added to chassis on a Ford motor car production line, 1909.** In 1908, Henry Ford began mass-producing a single type of car—the Model T Ford, which became known as the "Tin Lizzie".

Ford's methods brought down the price of a car and made it possible for many more people to own one. In 1910, he sold 18,664 Model T's, and in the years to come he was to sell 15 million.

In western countries, this new sort of society began to emerge towards the end of the 19th century. In Britain, Alfred Harmsworth (later Lord Northcliffe) recognized the trend and, in 1896 he produced the first popular daily newspaper, the *Daily Mail*.

Earlier newspapers had been aimed at the well-educated. The *Mail* was aimed at ordinary people and was soon selling over one million copies a day. William Hearst had a similar success with his *New York Journal*, launched in America in the same year. Their success stemmed from the growth of free education. Cheap books were produced too, and public libraries opened.

Mass production began with the Industrial Revolution, in the sense that the factory system led to the production of goods in increasing quantities. In the modern sense, however, it means more production of goods by teams of workers on an assembly line, rather than by skilled workers who make each product from start to finish. Henry Ford pioneered the method in the motor-car industry.

More food was a basic need of mass society. Increasing amounts of tinned food became available, and refrigeration now allowed meat to be transported long distances. Railways provided mass transport, and there were now motor buses, electric tramcars and underground railways as well. Edison's gramophone, and the new cinemas, provided mass entertainment.

Mass production meant mass marketing. This led to increased advertising and chain stores, at first in the grocery trade. In 1912, F.W. Woolworth opened his first "5 and 10 cent" store in the United States.

▲ **Advertisement for German margarine.** First produced in 1870, margarine was a scientific substitute for butter. It was made from animal fats, oils and skimmed milk, and it was a boon for the working classes for it was much cheaper than butter.

▲ **Charing Cross Station, London,** where underground, railway, bus, taxi and hansom cab met. Already, people were talking about London's traffic problem!

London's "Tube", opened in 1863, was the world's first underground railway. By 1910, it had extended to Shepherd's Bush, Hampstead, Finsbury Park and Balham. With the Tube added to motor buses and railways, people could now live outside the city and travel in to work. In 1900, one quarter of a million people were "commuting" daily into London.

School assembly. Free education was now available almost everywhere in the western world. It helped to create a mass society, for it began to break down the divisions between the rich and the poor.

Young worker in an American factory. The demand for machine hands at cheap rates of pay led to the employment of young people and women. They had provided factory labour since the earliest days of the Industrial Revolution.

Cinema show in America at the time of the Boer War. The early shows were given in converted shops and other premises and showed newsreels of interesting events. They helped to create a mass society, for thousands all over the world might see the same film.

French advertisement for a remedy for tired brains! Display advertisements were a feature of the popular press, and could be seen everywhere on hoardings. In the competition to establish brand names, Coca Cola, Player's Cigarettes and Bovril were already famous.

The Rise of America

▲ **Theodore "Teddy" Roosevelt on his ranch.**
He was the leader of a cavalry regiment during the Spanish–American War, and became a national hero. He was President of the United States from 1901-1909.

Roosevelt introduced laws to restrict the power of the big business trusts. He also proposed reforms in child labour and factory inspection, but these were blocked by powerful business interests in Congress.

▲ **Andrew Carnegie, head of the giant Carnegie Steel Company.** He was one of the most successful businessmen of the age. His business empire controlled, not only companies involved in the production of steel, but companies supplying raw materials for steel-making, and manufacturers of steel goods.

His methods were energetic and ruthless. In 1892, for example, his Company employed Pinkerton detectives to crush a strike of steel workers near Pittsburgh. The struggle developed into a bloody war that emphasized the divisions of American society.

▶ **Immigrants in a New York Street.** In the early years of the 20th century, immigration figures reached new heights. At this time, most of the new arrivals came from southern and eastern Europe: Poland, Italy, Austria–Hungary and Greece, for example.

No other country grew so rapidly in wealth and strength as America did from the end of the Civil War (1865) to 1900.

By 1900, the prairies and high plains of the American West had been settled by farmers and cattle ranchers. Railways spanned the continent and an intricate network linked the numerous cities of the East.

The cities themselves were growing. Throughout the 19th century, immigrants had been flooding into the United States, mainly from Europe. In 1860, no American city had a million inhabitants; by 1900, there were three—New York, Chicago and Philadelphia.

The United States was producing the basic needs of an industrial nation on a vast scale. In 1900, her output of coal and pig-iron exceeded that of Britain, her output of steel was greater than Germany's. She was also the world's leading producer of cotton, wheat and tobacco.

While many workers were underpaid and overworked, as in all industrial countries, "big business" thrived. Huge business "trusts" emerged; these were firms that banded together under a single committee to crush or buy up rival firms and control prices. Some men made huge fortunes—Andrew Carnegie in steel, for example, and John D. Rockefeller in oil.

As America grew in wealth, she began to expand overseas. "Our place must be great among nations", declared President Theodore Roosevelt. By the end of his term of office, the United States had acquired territories in the Pacific the Caribbean and in Latin America.

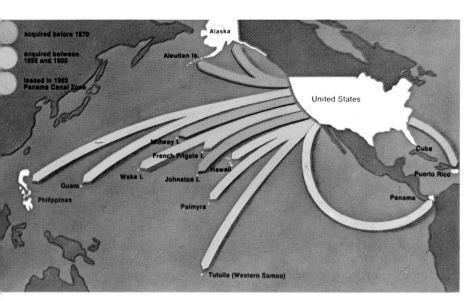

◀ **America's expansion overseas.** The United States had settled her own frontiers throughout the 19th century by purchase, war with Mexico and agreement with Britain. Now she gained territories abroad.

▼ **A Negro regiment in Cuba.** In 1898, the U.S. battleship *Maine* was blown up in the harbour at Havana, Cuba, where rebels had risen against the rule of Spain. At this, the United States declared war on Spain. The Spanish–American War lasted only four months.

A U.S. fleet routed a Spanish fleet in the Philippines and a second fleet was destroyed off Cuba. American troops soon occupied the island and Spain asked for peace.

The United States acquired the Philippines, Puerto Rico and Guam. Cuba became independent, with the United States acting as its protector.

Entertainment and Leisure

"What is the life of the rich man today?" asked a lady of the time. "A sort of firework!"

▲ **A travel poster advertises a shipping line.** By 1900, the moderately wealthy as well as the very rich could afford foreign travel. Thomas Cook had started his guided tours as early as 1841, when the coming of the railways had made travel cheaper. Carl Baedeker had published his first guide book even earlier, in 1839. Thereafter, no middle-class tourist would be seen abroad without his Baedeker clutched firmly in hand.

▲ **The beach at Scarborough in Yorkshire, 1900.** Rich and poor alike enjoyed holidays by the seaside. For the children there were donkey rides and Punch and Judy shows, for the adults, Pierrot shows and open-air concerts, as well as fun on the sands and in the sea. Swimming suits were less forbidding than in Victorian times, and mixed bathing was no longer frowned upon.

This, at one end of the social scale, was the life of people of the leisured class. They formed what would be called today an international "jet set", travelling from one centre of pleasure to another in comfort and style. At the gambling casino in Monte Carlo, you might with equal likelihood find a Russian prince, a French banker, a German count, an English lord or a wealthy American businessman.

At the other end of the scale was the working man. His weekend did not begin until lunch-time on Saturday and for him there was no paid annual holiday. If he took a week off in the summer to go with his family to the seaside, he did so by scrimping and saving throughout the year. Yet all save the poorest workers tried to take a holiday.

For workaday entertainment, people turned to the variety palaces. There were also the theatre and the opera for some, where the galleries provided cheap seats. At Christmas there were pantomimes.

Later, the cinema arrived as a popular form of mass entertainment, and by 1913, variety palaces everywhere were being turned into cinemas. The first films had been newsreels, but in 1903 came the first full-length "story" on the screen, *The Great Train Robbery*. It lasted twelve minutes.

For many, sport now provided an absorbing leisure activity—either as spectators or as active participants. "I cannot imagine a world with little or no football, tennis, hockey, golf, croquet and cycling, despite the fact that all these recreations are the growth and invention of less than half a century" said an English writer in 1903. In England, low-paid workers had become supporters of their local soccer teams and the F.A. Cup Final of 1908 was watched by 75,000 people.

Cover of a programme for the *Palace Theatre of Varieties* **in London.**

At music-halls, men drank and ate while watching a wide variety of acts, from circus performers to stand-up comics telling *risqué* stories. Women did not attend music-halls, but they did go to the palaces of variety which took their place and which did not have bars.

At the "variety" you might see famous actors appearing in an excerpt from a play as well as jugglers, tumblers, dancers, comics, male and female impersonators, singers or ventriloquists. Four of the best-known performers were Marie Lloyd, Dan Leno, Harry Lauder and the famous escapologist, Harry Houdini.

▲ Poster advertising *Lippincott's*, a magazine which first appeared in the United States in the late 19th century. Others included *Harper's Bazaar* and *Scribner's Magazine*. A new public, avid for reading matter, was emerging. In England, *Tit-Bits* (1881), *Answers* (1888) and *Pearson's Weekly* (1890) flourished. By 1910 there were 2,785 newspapers and journals in Britain.

◀ **Poster for the** *Folies Bergère* **in Paris,** which opened in 1869 as a music-hall. By 1900, it was making a name for itself with its extravagant and varied programmes. As public tolerance grew, the *Folies* began to present scantily-dressed and later nude girls as features of its shows, and in time it became identified by these.

Colonial Africa

Africa is the second largest continent in the world. It was colonized with astonishing speed during the late 19th century.

▲ **Henry Morton Stanley,** one of the greatest of all African explorers. A journalist, he was sent to find Livingstone in 1869 and, after finding him, became interested in Africa. In 1874-7 he discovered the source of the Congo River. He made his last visit in 1897.

The "Dark Continent" had been opened up during the 19th century by missionaries and explorers, men like Livingstone, Stanley, Burton, Speke and Baker. By 1900, the map of Africa had been drawn, and most of the continent had been divided between the European powers. In 1875, one tenth of Africa had been colonized. Less than 20 years later, the only independent states were Liberia and Ethiopia.

The industrial countries of Europe wanted colonies in Africa to provide themselves with raw materials, minerals and food. They also wanted markets for their own manufactured goods. Yet there was another motive behind the spread of "imperialism"; it was the desire of nations for the "prestige" of possessing overseas colonies.

There was always a danger of clashes between the colonial powers. In 1898, British and French forces faced each other on the Nile at Fashoda, as rivals for the control of Egypt. But a peaceful solution was found to this problem as it was to others. Usually, each side was ready to make concessions.

Nor was there much violent resistance from Africans. British troops crushed a nationalist army to win control of the Sudan. Germany had two wars with the local peoples in South-West Africa in 1904-1907, and in East Africa in 1905. At the battle of Adowa (1898) in Ethiopia, however, Africans successfully repelled a European power when they defeated the Italians.

▲ **The Battle of Omdurman, 1898,** in which British forces led by General Kitchener defeated over 70,000 fanatical Dervishes. The victory added the Sudan to the British Empire.

This vast area on the headwaters of the Nile had previously been under Egyptian and British rule but was lost to the Dervishes in 1884 when General Gordon was killed at Khartoum. At that time, British interest in the region was not great. But by the end of the century, Egypt and the Sudan were key links in Britain's African empire.

▶ **How the scramble for Africa ended:** by 1914, only Ethiopia and Liberia remained independent. Old European rivalries emerged during the scramble. Germany joined in to obtain a "place in the sun" like France and Britain and wound up with colonies that she did not really want.

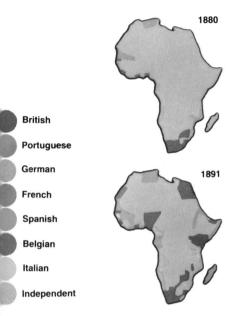

1880

1891

British

Portuguese

German

French

Spanish

Belgian

Italian

Independent

Africa 1914

Algeria 1830
Morocco 1912
Morocco 1911
Ifni 1860
Rio de Oro 1885
French West Africa 1909
Gambia 1816
Guinea 1866
Sierra Leone 1737
Liberia Independent 1847
Ivory Coast 1893
Gold Coast 1874
Togoland 1884
Nigeria 1885-1900
Guinea 1842
Cameroons 1884
French Congo 1885
Belgian Congo 1908
Angola 1576
Nyasaland 1891
Rhodesia 1899
Walvis Bay 1878
German South-West Africa 1884
Bechuanaland 1885

Tunisia 1881
Tripoli 1912
Egypt 1914
Anglo-Egyptian Sudan 1889
French Somaliland 1802
British Somaliland 1884
Eritrea 1890
Italian Somaliland 1889
Ethiopia Independent
British East Africa 1895
Zanzibar 1890
German East Africa 1890
Madagascar 1642
Portuguese East Africa 1506
Transvaal 1902
Natal 1843
Orange Free State 1902
Cape Colony 1814

▲ **Marshall Louis Lyautey,** French colonial administrator, in Arab dress. He built up a chain of outposts in the borderlands of Algeria and Morocco to provide protection for the tribes against raiders.

In 1912, when Morocco became a protectorate of France, Lyautey was made resident-general. At once, he began to organize the country, building roads and founding schools and hospitals. A country of scattered tribes became a unity. This was colonialism at its best.

◀ **African women in chains in the so-called Congo Free State.** This was ruled by King Leopold II of Belgium. He made it his personal possession and made laws to ensure that practically all the ivory and wild rubber came to him.

Villages were taxed in work, mainly in the collection of rubber. When natives tried to avoid working they were killed or mutilated. In the 1900's, after an outcry in Europe, the Congo was taken from Leopold and handed over to the Belgian government.

23

The Boer War

▲ **Paul Kruger, President of the Transvaal.**
Fanatically hostile to Britain, he had imported
German arms in preparation for the war that
was to drive the British out of South Africa. In
1900, he fled to Europe to seek help. At one
stage, the Kaiser threatened to send troops to
the aid of the Boers. Holland, France and
Russia were all critical of Britain, for it
appeared that the mighty British Empire was
waging war against a small country with few
armed forces. Yet in the end, *Oom Paul* (Uncle
Paul), as Kruger was nicknamed, obtained no
help at all.

**Rich gold-fields were discovered in the Boer republic of the
Traansvaal in southern Africa in 1886. People flocked there and
the high taxes they paid enriched the republic.**

The Boers called the gold-seekers
Uitlanders (foreigners), and refused to
grant them equal rights as citizens. The
Uitlanders protested strongly, supported by Britain, since many of the
Uitlanders were British. But the Boers
would not meet British demands for
fairer treatment for the Uitlanders. Instead, in October 1899, the Transvaal
declared war on Britain. The Orange
Free State, another Boer republic,
joined them.

At first, the British, with only 15,000
troops in South Africa, were outnumbered. By December, the Boers
were besieging the towns of Kimberley,
Ladysmith and Mafeking. In January
1900, however, fresh troops from Britain
arrived with a new commander, Lord
Roberts, and Lord Kitchener as his
chief-of-staff. Troops also arrived from
Australia, New Zealand and Canada,
and the Boers, with 65,000 men, were
outnumbered.

In February, Kimberley and Ladysmith were relieved and the British
pressed on into the Orange Free State
and the Transvaal. Meantime, Mafeking was relieved after a siege lasting
217 days.

The Boers fell back on guerilla war
waged by small groups called com-
mandos. They finally made peace in
May, 1902. The Transvaal and the
Orange Free State became colonies of
Britain, but the Boers were given £3m
to help them repair their homes and
farms.

▼ **A Boer on horseback.** *Boer* is a Dutch word meaning farmer, and was the name given to the descendents of the Dutch settlers in South Africa. Since most were still farmers, they were fine horsemen and, knowing the country, became skilled guerillas.

▲ **Lord Kitchener looming over dead Boers in a French cartoon.** British commander from 1901, he put Boer women and children in prison camps "to avoid bloodshed". Yet over 20,000 of them died in the camps from diseases like pneumonia, measles and enteric fever. His policy heightened anti-British feeling abroad.

▼ **British troops crossing a river under fire.** The rough country and the hot climate caused problems to the British. Only 6,000 troops died in battle; 16,000 died from disease. Transport was difficult. "The English never leave the railway, so they cannot make turning movements", commented one Boer general.

The British and India

▲ **Maharajah of Kanwar** and a British official in an egg-and-spoon race. Indian princes were accepted as social equals. They flocked to the viceroy's court for various functions.

India in 1900 was Britain's largest imperial possession, a source of wealth, power and prestige.

At this time, the British had controlled the vast sub-continent of India for nearly half a century. The East India Company had taken over the peninsula bit by bit. Then, following the Indian Mutiny of 1857, the British Government took over directly. Queen Victoria appointed a viceroy to govern India, and, under him, an army of 5,000 officials had the formidable task of running a continent with 300 million inhabitants.

Within India, there were seven provinces with an English official in charge of each. There was also a large number of states ruled by Indian princes who gave their allegiance to Britain. The viceroy could intervene in the native states in the event of mis-government.

Britain obtained much-needed imports from India, including cotton and tea, while the sub-continent provided a huge market for manufactured goods in return. The British brought more than their manufactured goods, however. They built up the world's largest railway network and set up postal and telegraph services. They irrigated areas of barren land and provided drainage in the cities to offset insanitary conditions. They introduced an education system including universities attended by a large number of upper-class Indians. Yet by 1900, resentment against British rule and demands for independence were growing.

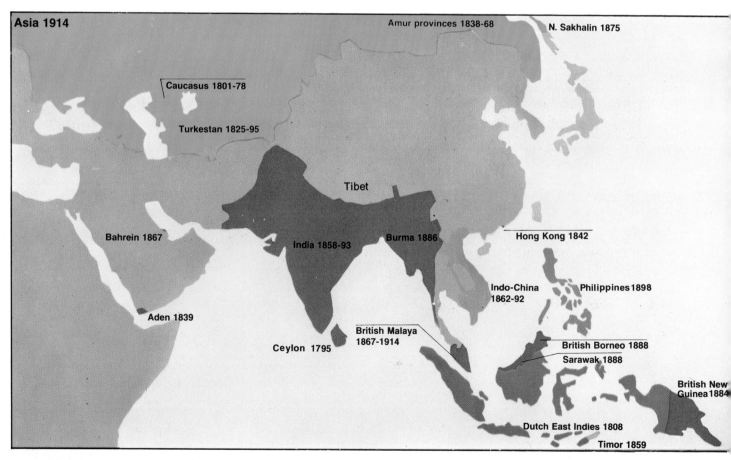

Asia 1914

Amur provinces 1838-68

N. Sakhalin 1875

Caucasus 1801-78

Turkestan 1825-95

Tibet

Bahrein 1867

India 1858-93

Burma 1886

Hong Kong 1842

Indo-China 1862-92

Philippines 1898

Aden 1839

British Malaya 1867-1914

Ceylon 1795

British Borneo 1888

Sarawak 1888

British New Guinea 1884

Dutch East Indies 1808

Timor 1859

▲ **How the powers divided up the East.** The biggest prize was India, and this became part of the British Empire (red) with Burma adding a vast eastern area in 1886. France (mauve) acquired Indo-China, and the United States (purple) took the Philippines from Spain. Just as Britain took over India from the British East India Company, so Holland (brown) took over the Dutch East India Company which had operated in the islands since 1602. Russia (green) also had a large appetite.

The colonization of the East, however, was not as complete as in Africa. China retained her independence, and Japan was already considered to be a world power.

▲ **A loyal subject of the British Empire with portraits of King George V and Queen Mary.** They travelled to India in 1911 for a *durbar* (ceremonial meeting) in which they received the homage of the Indian princes. It was a glittering event. But, already, Hindu and Moslem groups were working to free India.

◀ **British official in India takes his ease.** Note the servants: one carries a large fan while another attends to his master's feet. Yet life was not all a round of leisure for British officials. Apart from normal business, flood and famine often posed problems. Between 1866-1900, there were four major famines in which nine million people died.

▲ **Medal for the British invasion of Tibet,** 1903-4, with a photograph of a Tibetan shot by the British. The poorly equipped Tibetans opposed a large and modern British force.

Tibet

Early in the 20th century, Russia showed an interest in Tibet, the remote land in the high mountains to the north of India. At this, the British sent a mission from India into Tibet with an armed escort. It fought its way to the capital, the "forbidden city" of Lhasa, under the leadership of Lieut. Col. (later Sir) Francis Younghusband in 1904.

The ruler of Tibet, the Dalai Lama, had fled to Mongolia but Younghusband made a treaty with his deputies. By this, Tibet promised not to make treaties with any other country without British permission.

China had long claimed overlordship of Tibet and had to be consulted. In 1907, both Britain and Russia recognized China's rights and agreed to stay out of Tibet. An armed Chinese expedition reached Lhasa in 1910, and the Dalai Lama was again forced to flee. But in 1911, the Chinese Empire was overthrown and a republic set up. Chinese troops in Tibet fell into disorder and were driven out. The Dalai Lama returned once more.

China: the Boxer Rising

▼ **An accused man grovels on the floor before a judge in a Chinese court.** From 1644, China was ruled by the Manchu emperors. For centuries, life changed very little. Most people were farmers.

"Protect the country! Destroy the foreigners!" In 1900, a secret society launched a rising in China. It was the I-ho Ch'uan, the Society of Righteous and Harmonious Fists.

Members of the society were popularly known as Boxers. They believed that they could become possessed by spirits and, in this state, could suffer no injury from swords or bullets. Their aim was to drive foreigners and their influence out of China.

Throughout the 19th century, the great powers of Europe had acquired trading rights in Chinese seaports and areas of the country. Sometimes, as in the British acquisition of Hong Kong, the European gains came as a result of war. In time, Britain, France and Russia controlled areas of the old Chinese Empire, and, along with Germany, had their own areas of influence as well. By 1899, it looked as if China itself might be split up among the foreigners.

The imperial dynasty was weak. Belated attempts to modernize the country along western lines were crushed in 1898 when the Empress Dowager Tzu-hsi came to the throne.

Then came the Rising. The Boxers attacked foreigners and Chinese Christians (there was much missionary activity in China at this time). Hundreds were killed in the provinces, and many fled to the capital, Peking.

There was a compound in the city, containing the legations—or residences and offices—of foreign officials. The compound was about eleven acres in extent and normally housed some 60 people. It was to these legations that the refugees retired, and soon there were over 3,000 Chinese Christians, 475 foreign civilians and 450 marines barricaded in the compound.

By this time, the Empress and the government were openly supporting the Boxers. On 20 June 1900, the Boxers, helped by Chinese troops, opened fire on the legations and a siege began. It lasted for 55 days before a force made up of troops from eight nations fought its way into the city. Peace was made on 7 December 1901. China had to pay $33m in compensation to foreign countries.

Tz'u-hsi, Empress of China at the time of the Rising. She supported the Boxers against foreigners and, on 21 June 1900, declared war on the European powers. This act cost China dearly.

Admiral Sir Edward Seymour set out for Peking with a force of 2,000 men before the siege began. They travelled by train, and attacks by Boxers on the line slowed progress to a crawl. Seymour turned back.

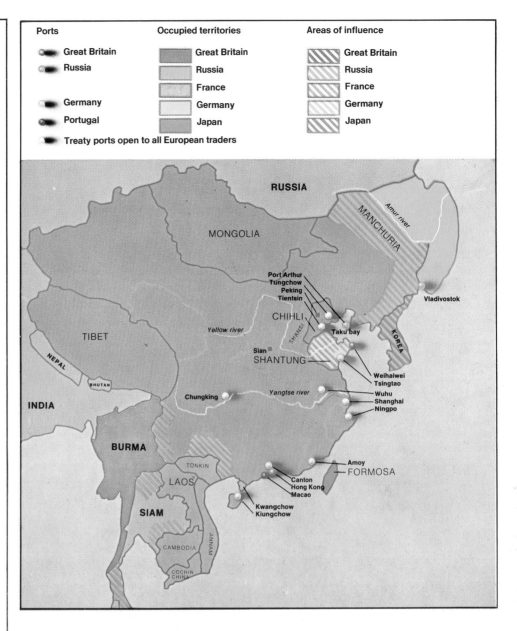

Ports	Occupied territories	Areas of influence
Great Britain	Great Britain	Great Britain
Russia	Russia	Russia
Germany	France	France
Portugal	Germany	Germany
	Japan	Japan
Treaty ports open to all European traders		

▲ **How the great powers of Europe, and Japan, encroached on the Chinese Empire.** They wanted places to sell their manufactured goods. In return, they wanted China's produce.

Japan's quarrel with China over Korea led to war in 1894-5. China was defeated in several battles within her own frontiers, and was forced to grant Korea's independence and give Formosa to Japan. Russia, France and Germany protested about other concessions to Japan and a further scramble for trading rights in China took place.

▲ This picture, put out by the Boxers, shows **European troops retreating before the Boxers.** It appealed to most Chinese because all save Chinese Christians hated the foreigners. Yet the Boxers' lawlessness made them unpopular with their own countrymen.

▲ **The fate of a Boxer after the Rising.** Beheading remained a punishment in China along with many medieval customs. World War I began what is still a continuing process —the industrialization of China.

Japan Expands

▲ **Japanese students in Western-style clothes.** Their abrupt change from traditional dress reflected the social changes in Japan.

Japan had opened some of her ports to foreign trade in 1854. Under the rule of Emperor Meiji Tenno, from 1868 to 1912, Japan absorbed the influence of the west.

New laws were passed to modernize Japan along western lines. Compulsory education was introduced, and the old restrictions preventing Japanese going abroad were removed. The first railway was built in 1872, and by the 1890's, Japan had large and flourishing factories and shipyards. Japan became a dynamic industrial nation within a single generation.

Then, needing more food and raw materials, Japan looked for colonies and cast greedy eyes on Korea. But China had claims on Korea, and war followed in 1894-5. In this, Japan defeated China; it was the victory of a country that had modernized successfully over one which

had failed. Japan was given the island of Formosa, and Korea was allowed to come under her influence.

Japan now became worried about Russian influence in the decaying Chinese Empire. Russia had moved troops into Manchuria during the Boxer Rising, and failed to remove them long after the Rising was suppressed. She also had designs on Korea.

Japan was prepared to tolerate Russian influence in Manchuria, if Russia would accept Japanese supremacy in Korea. Russia would make no such concessions. In the war that followed, in 1904-5, Japan was again dramatically successful.

▲ **The opening of the first imperial parliament:** the Emperor hands out an imperial edict to the Prime Minister, Ito Hirobumi. In 1889, Japan was given a Western-style constitution.

▶ **Japanese textile factory at the turn of the century.** The Japanese textile industry grew quickly because it was possible to sell goods in China and Korea.

The shortage of raw materials held up the development of some industries. For example, the shortage of iron ore and coking coal prevented the rapid expansion of the steel industry. Yet the output of coal was trebled within ten years.

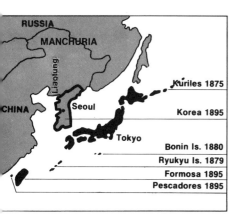

▲ **Japan's gains prior to the Russo–Japanese War of 1904-5.** After the war, the Russians gave up their claims to Korea and also handed over part of Manchuria.

▲ **Port Arthur on the Liaotung Peninsula under fire** from the Japanese in the Russo–Japanese War. Russia lost this key seaport.

◄ **Russian gunners relax at Port Arthur.** In a full-scale war, Tsarist forces proved no match for those of westernized Japan.

▼ **Japanese sailors in action at the battle of Tsushima.** Here, the Japanese fleet, under the command of Admiral Togo, destroyed the Russian 2nd squadron. Coming shortly after the Russian defeat at Port Arthur, Tsushima sealed the Russians' fate. The western world was astonished by the Japanese victory.

The Tsar's Russia

When Nicholas II was crowned Tsar of the vast Russian Empire in 1894, he took over a troubled land.

▲ **Tsar Nicholas II and his wife,** Alexandra of Hesse-Darmstadt, grand-daughter of Queen Victoria. Handsome, gentle and religious, Nicholas was dominated by Alexandra.

Tsar Peter the Great had set out to westernize Russia two centuries earlier, and, since then, a great deal of progress had been made. Russia had technical schools and universities, a few flourishing industries and thriving trade.

Yet Russia was still largely a land of peasants, living in conditions that had not much changed since the Middle Ages. The tsars had, for centuries, depended on the land-owning nobles and the Russian Orthodox Church for their power. Nicholas II hoped to rule like all the tsars before him, as an autocrat, making his own laws and taking all national decisions.

Now, however, the tsars' time seemed to be running out. Nicholas II's grandfather had been assassinated in 1881, and his father had kept order only by brutal tyranny. A new class of citizens had emerged—educated people of the middle classes.

There were serious peasant disorders in 1902-4, and in 1904-5, all of Russia was upset by the disaster of the Russo-Japanese War. Demands for a new form of rule grew stronger.

Then came "Bloody Sunday", 22 January 1905. An orderly protest demonstration was fired on by troops and hundreds died. Months of disorder followed. Peasants rioted, workers, professional men, even schoolchildren went on strike. The tsar agreed to introduce a form of parliament elected by the people.

In 1906, elections were held and the *Duma* (parliament) was formed. Yet, before it met, Nicholas limited its powers. The *Duma* had some influence but no real authority over affairs in Russia. By 1913, tsardom looked like surviving. Then events led Nicholas to plunge into The Great War, which brought both Russia and himself to ultimate disaster.

▲ **Russian stamp commemorating the battleship** *Potemkin* **mutiny, 1905.** It is remembered today as a great victory in the struggle for freedom from the yoke of the tsars. Yet the crew did not rebel for political reasons.

▶ **Workers defending a barricade in a street in Moscow, 23 December 1905.** This rising was organized by a council of workers in the city.

On 30 October 1905, the Tsar had signed the "October Manifesto" promising a form of elected parliament. The workers were not satisfied: they wanted a democratic republic. In November, there was a call for a general strike. The response, however, was poor and 300 workers were arrested. The Moscow rising in December was the workers' last throe and it was soon put down.

Count Sergei Witte (left), a one-time station-master who rose to become adviser to the Tsar. He advised Nicholas to sign the "October Manifesto", but regarded it only as a device for halting the 1905 Revolution. He said, "I have a constitution in my head, but, as to my heart, I spit on it."

Peter Stolypin (right), Prime Minister of Russia 1906-11, devoted himself to staving off revolution, chiefly by helping the peasants. He arranged for them to have their land in single plots instead of in pieces scattered around their village. He also encouraged them to use the Land Bank. He was murdered in 1911.

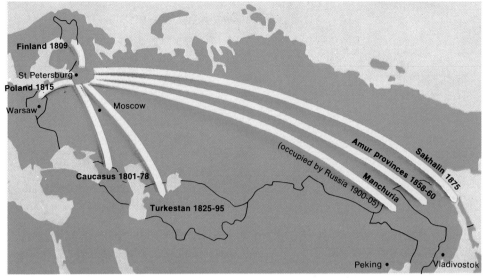

▲ **Throughout the 19th century, Russia had expanded her frontiers,** and, between 1900 and 1905, she occupied Manchuria. In Nicholas II's time, less than half of the Russian Empire's population was Russian. The Trans-Siberian Railway was built to link the heart of Russia with Vladivostock, far in the east. Begun in 1891, it was not finally completed until 1917.

◀ **Market day in a provincial Russian town. 90% of the population still worked the land.**

▼ **Family of *kulaks* (well-to-do peasants) drinking tea from a *samovar* (tea urn).**

The peasants

Until 1861, over half of Russia's peasants had been serfs, the personal property of private landowners. Few of the rest were any better off, living on land belonging to the Tsar and having to fulfil various conditions and duties.

The end of serfdom did not solve all the problems of the peasantry. Some peasants became tenant farmers with too little land to make a living. Many were burdened by the taxes which they had to pay to their old owners in compensation for their release.

Yet others did well. They borrowed money from the Peasants' Land Bank, set up in 1883, and, in time formed a new, wealthy class of peasants known as *kulaks*.

Labour Unrest

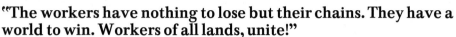

"The workers have nothing to lose but their chains. They have a world to win. Workers of all lands, unite!"

▲ **Unemployed workers in Britain,** victims of an industrial society only just beginning to care for them. But better times were coming—pensions, sick pay and unemployment pay for some workers were provided by 1911, as well as some free medical treatment. This was the start of the Welfare State.

Rise in German Trade Union Membership

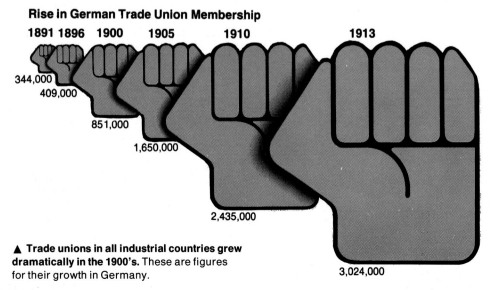

| 1891 | 1896 | 1900 | 1905 | 1910 | 1913 |

344,000
409,000
851,000
1,650,000
2,435,000
3,024,000

▲ **Trade unions in all industrial countries grew dramatically in the 1900's.** These are figures for their growth in Germany.

These words end the Communist Manifesto, one of the great revolutionary works of the 19th century. By 1900, they had wide appeal.

The Industrial Revolution had created a new class of people who owned little property and had only their labour to sell. It was they who made the goods on which the wealth of advanced countries was built; yet they received little share of that wealth.

Employers seemed to care very little for them. The take-over of a firm, a cutback in production or the introduction of labour-saving machinery might at any time mean a reduction in employment. Workers lived in dread of being "turned off". They were at the mercy of the ups and downs of trade, for if a company went out of business, thousands might be put out of work.

There were many fluctuations in world trade in the early 1900's, and mass unemployment was a problem that all industrial nations had to face. Some governments did try to tackle the problem; in Britain, for example, labour exchanges were introduced in 1909, to help the unemployed find jobs.

But, by now, many had lost faith in governments. Trade unions grew apace. They had often used strikes to try and win better wages or terms of employment. Now, however, the scope and gravity of strike action was increasing.

Governments had sometimes used police or soldiers to crush strikes; now in many countries, strikes were used to try and influence or even bring down governments. There were general strikes in Russia (1904-5), Holland (1903), Sweden (1902 and 1909), Italy (1900, 1904-5 and 1911) and Belgium (1913). Attempts were even made to introduce an international one-day strike on 1 May every year, to demonstrate the unity of the labour movement throughout the world.

▶ **Italian workers on strike in 1905.** This was a particularly tense year of unrest in Italy.

Socialists and Anarchists

While striking workers struggled for a better life, some people sought to change society as a whole.

Two groups in particular caused much alarm to the wealthy—the socialists and the anarchists. Both believed that industries should be owned by the people who worked in them, rather than by private businessmen. Similarly, the land should be owned by the people who tilled the soil, rather than by a few landowners. Both believed that existing governments and laws served to protect property-owners against the rightful demands of the workers.

Anarchists challenged the principle of government itself. They believed that laws and the habit of private ownership had corrupted people; people would willingly work for the common good if authority, whether that of kings, politicians, priests, or businessmen, could be overthrown.

In the late 19th century, anarchists pursued their aims by random acts of terrorism. They threw bombs in public places and assassinated political leaders.

Later, as they failed to win mass support, they became active in the trade union movement. Anarchists particularly favoured general strikes.

Socialists organized themselves into political parties. There was also an organization called the Second International, that linked the parties of different countries. By 1913 it claimed many millions of members, and it was hoped that it would be strong enough to prevent governments from involving their workers in wars. The outbreak of World War One brought this dream, and the Second International with it, to ruins.

There were differences between socialists of different countries. In Russia, for example, the workers had few rights and socialists therefore tended to be violent revolutionaries. In Britain, where the government was less repressive, socialists formed a Labour Party and some of its members were elected to Parliament.

▲ **The assassination of Carnot,** 24 June 1894. Returning from a public banquet, Marie-François Carnot, President of France, was stabbed by an anarchist at Lyons. He died almost at once. "The mad dog is the closest parallel in nature to the anarchist" commented a writer in a British magazine of the time.

▲ **The assassination of William McKinley, President of the United States.** He was shot by an anarchist at an exhibition in Buffalo on 6 September 1901. He died eight days later. "Anarchism is a crime against the human race" declared the new president, Theodore Roosevelt.

▲ **James Keir Hardie,** Britain's first socialist M.P. He worked in a Scottish coal mine from the age of ten to twenty, and later became a journalist. He was elected to Parliament in 1892 and turned up in a check suit and a cloth hat instead of formal dress. He was the first chairman of the Independent Labour Party, precursor of the Labour Party.

▲ Police file on **Vladimir Ilyich Ulyanov** who changed his name to Lenin. He grew up in the Russia of Tsar Alexander III where unions were not tolerated. He was later sent to Siberia for forming one. From 1900 Lenin lived outside Russia, striving to organize a revolutionary socialist party to overthrow the Tsar. He returned to Russia briefly after the 1905 rising.

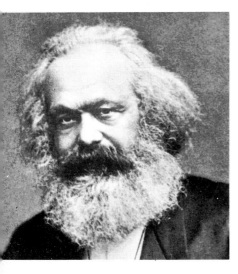

▲ **Karl Marx,** German-born author of *The Communist Manifesto* and *Das Kapital*. His theories were the inspiration of most continental socialists by 1900. He had been the secretary of the First International Working Men's Association.

How they differed

Socialists and anarchists shared many common goals, yet they disagreed strongly on some matters. Socialists accepted the discipline of party organization. They often stood in elections, and, in France, a socialist even entered a government (though this scandalized many of his colleagues).

Anarchists mistrusted all political activity and refused to stand in elections. They were hard to organize, for rules and regulations were among the very things they wished to overthrow. Broadly, anarchists were strongest in peasant countries, socialists in industrial ones.

▼ **Rioting strikers confront the police in France.** Notice the red flag of the socialists and the black flag of the anarchists.

▲ **Prince Peter Kropotkin,** a Russian aristocrat who became an anarchist. He called for "permanent revolt by word of mouth, in writing, by the dagger, by rifle, by dynamite". He was imprisoned in Russia and France.

Aviation

Inventors had already experimented with balloons and gliders; the first powered flight in a heavier-than-air craft was made by Orville Wright in December 1903.

This historic event failed to create a sensation. Few newspapers reported it, for editors suspected that the report was exaggerated, or a hoax. As Orville and his brother, Wilbur, did not make a public flight until 1908, the possibility of manned and powered flight seemed to most people to be no more than a fanciful dream.

Other pioneers were, however, experimenting with aircraft of various kinds in several countries. Alberto Santos-Dumont made the first flights in Europe in 1906, in a machine of his own design. But the Europeans had a lot to learn from the Wright brothers and when, in 1908, Wilbur travelled to France to give demonstrations, they learned their lessons well. In the years that followed, aviation made good progress.

In 1909, Louis Blériot caused a sensation by flying the English Channel in a monoplane that he had designed himself. Later, air meetings were held on both sides of the Atlantic and then, in 1911, came a series of thrilling cross-country races: Paris–Madrid, Paris–Rome, Circuit of Europe and Circuit of Britain.

Public interest was now enormous. When Henri Jullerot put on a display at Calcutta, for example, it was watched by 75,000 people.

Meantime, governments were recognizing the military possibilities of aviation. In 1908-13, Germany and France each spent over £5 million on military aviation. Before World War One began, aircraft had already been used in war. In 1911, during the Italo-Turkish War, an Italian pilot made the first reconaissance on enemy positions from one, and, in 1912, in the Balkan War, Bulgarian aircraft dropped finned canisters of explosives on the Turks at Adrianople.

▲ **Louis Blériot and his wife.** When he landed near Dover on 25 July 1909, he set a problem for the Customs, as no one had ever entered Britain by aeroplane before. An official, being used to ships, put Blériot down on his form as being the captain of a vessel described as a monoplane.

▲ **The first powered flight.** Orville is in the biplane, known as *Flyer,* and Wilbur is alongside it. The two brothers were bicycle makers from Dayton, Ohio, and they built their first petrol-driven aircraft after four years of experiments with kites and gliders. On the day of the first flight, both brothers made several other flights in turn. The longest lasted 59 seconds, in which the *Flyer* flew 852 feet (260m).

The *Flyer* was an experimental machine. The first practical aircraft was the *Flyer III* of 1905, which could bank, turn and circle, and fly for about half an hour at 35m.p.h. (56k.p.h.). Wilbur made flights lasting up to two hours 20 minutes in 1908, and soon Wright biplanes were being built on licence in Britain, France and Germany.

The B.E.2a, designed by Geoffrey de ...illand and built at the Royal Aircraft ...tory. It made its first appearance in 1912 ...was Britain's top military aircraft at the ...reak of World War One. Yet it lacked ...noeuvrability, and this fault was to lead to ...alling casualities.
...pan: 38ft 7½in (11.8m). Length: 29ft 9½in ...m). Top speed: 70 m.p.h. (112.65 k.p.h.). ...nb rate: 9 minutes to 3,000ft (914m).

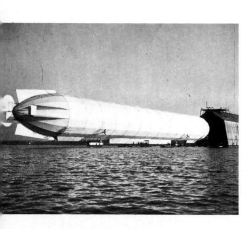

...erman rigid airship LZ4, nicknamed ...ppelin'' after the designer, Count ...dinand von Zeppelin. Zeppelins were used ...art the world's first airline between cities, ...ermany in 1910.
...t this time, many people believed that the ...re of air transport lay with airships, and ...many saw them as major weapons of war.

...oster for French air display, 1910. In ...–14, there were many meetings of this ...and various other events, as more ...raft became available and more people ...up flying.
...y the end of 1912, 966 aviator's certificates ...been issued in France, and 382 in Britain.

Revolution in the Arts

▲ **Picasso's** *Les Demoiselles d'Avignon* **(1907),** perhaps the earliest example of truly 20th century art. In it, he broke with two major features of previous European painting: the naturalistic proportions of the human figure, and the illusion of perspective from a single point.

▼ *Elasticity* **(1912) by Umberto Boccioni, an early example of abstract painting.**

"A roaring motor car which runs like a machine-gun is more beautiful than the Winged Victory of Samothrace."

Ideas like this one, expressed by an Italian "Futurist", staggered the art-loving public at the start of the 20th century. The arts were becoming increasingly free and experimental.

At this time, Paris was the most influential centre for the visual arts. Already at the end of the 19th century, Cézanne, Gauguin and Toulouse-Lautrec had produced less naturalistic, more self-conscious styles of painting. All three aimed for the greatest possible simplicity, and used strong, bright colours. This was taken a step further by the *Fauves* (wild beasts) of whom the best known is Henri Matisse.

At the same time, Pablo Picasso, Georges Braque and others were developing an approach to painting which became known as "Cubism". This laid stress on the structure as well as the surface appearance of objects, and it paved the way for the more revolutionary abstract art developed by Wassily Kan-

dinsky. He finished his first wholly abstract painting in 1910.

In sculpture, Auguste Rodin produced increasingly free forms, and Jacob Epstein made further breaks with tradition.

Equally bewildering to the public were the musical experiments of Debussy, Schoenberg and Stravinsky. Schoenberg's Chamber Symphony caused a riot at its first performance in 1907, and, in 1913, Stravinsky's ballet *The Rite of Spring* roused the audience to fury.

▲ **A Dutch tobacco shop decorated in** *art nouveau* **style.** *Art nouveau* (new art) was a decorative style that became fashionable from the 1880's. It affected applied arts such as interior decoration, typography, book illustration, jewellery, ceramics and even architecture. Its main feature was the swirling movement that it evoked. The swaying patterns suggest flames or the sweeping movement of waves, seaweed or growing plants. In this building, even the shelves are curved.

◀ **Costume designed by Bakst for a dancer in the** *Ballets Russes,* a legendary company run by the Russian impresario Sergei Diaghilev. He first presented dancers from Russia in Paris in 1909. Two years later he formed a permanent company with headquarters in Monte Carlo. From there, the company regularly toured Europe, always triumphantly.

The finest painters and musicians of the day contributed to the success of the *Ballets* as well as two of the greatest dancers of all time, Pavlova and Nijinsky. Stravinsky composed music for several ballets.

▲ **The influence of cubism can be seen in this sculpture by Jacob Epstein,** *The Rock Drill* **(1913).** It also reflects an enthusiasm for mechanization not uncommon at this time.

Epstein became famous in 1910 when he completed 18 enormous figures on the British Medical Association Building in London, representing man and woman in their various stages from birth to old age. They provoked anger, one newspaper describing them as ''a form of statuary which no careful father would wish his daughter, and no discriminating young man his fiancée, to see''.

Ships and Seapower

▲ **Poster for an American shipping company.**
During the first years of the 20th century,
British superiority in shipping came into
fierce competition. Foreign liners and
merchant ships challenged British ones on
all the major routes.

By the end of the 19th century, the doom of the sailing ship was sealed.

The last of the big clippers still carried wool to Britain from Australia, and, until the opening of the Panama Canal in 1915, windjammers carried grain from the west coast of the United States to the east.

But this was the age of steam. Steamships were more reliable than sailing ships, for they were not at the mercy of the winds. On the oceans of the world, the paddle wheel had long given way to the screw, and ships were no longer built of wood but of iron, and, later, steel.

In 1897, Charles Parsons invented a new type of steam engine for ships. Instead of using steam to push a lever which turned a wheel, he produced an engine in which steam itself turned the wheel. The engine, called the steam turbine, allowed ships to be driven much faster. The turbine-driven *Mauretania*, for example, crossed the Atlantic at 26 knots in 1907.

Steamships still used coal as a fuel, and taking it on was a dirty and laborious business. Oil was not often used until after World War One.

Great merchant fleets carried manufactured goods all over the world. They returned with raw materials for the factories and food for the people crowded into the expanding cities. Meanwhile, luxury liners competed for the growing tourist trade. After the sinking of the *Titanic*, new safety measures were introduced.

▼ **Britain's Royal Navy Review at Spithead in 1898.** In the late 19th century, France and Russia, who were allies, built up their navies; Britain's strategy was to have a navy equal to the combined strengths of the French and Russian navies. In 1898, Germany launched her new naval programme, a determined assault on British supremacy.

"God Himself could not sink this ship," a steward told a nervous lady boarding a new liner at Southampton on 10 April 1912. It was the *Titanic*, the largest, and, it was thought, the safest steamship afloat. She had an extra bottom inside her steel hull, and many other safety devices.

Yet, on the night of 14–15 April, far out in the North Atlantic, the *Titanic* struck an iceberg and sank. In spite of radio messages, 1,513 of the 2,208 people aboard died in the freezing waters before help arrived. After this tragedy, ships had to carry enough lifeboats for everybody. Iceberg patrols started and ships kept 24-hour radio watches.

▼ **British Super Dreadnought, H.M.S.** *Queen Elizabeth,* **launched in 1913.** The design of the Dreadnought was based on lessons learnt in the Russo–Japanese War. Dreadnoughts carried more big, long-range guns than earlier vessels, and fewer secondary armaments. Some, like the *Queen Elizabeth,* were to serve in World War Two as well as World War One.

The Naval Race

In the early 1900's, the four major naval powers were Britain, France, Japan and the United States. The United States won two overwhelming victories in the Spanish–American war of 1898 without losing a ship, and, afterwards, President "Teddy" Roosevelt began to build up the U.S. Navy.

Japan's new strength was shown when she beat Russia in the Battle of Tsushima in 1905. One year later, Britain built the ultimate battleship—H.M.S. *Dreadnought,* a huge, iron-plated ship of 17,000 tons. She had ten 12-inch guns and 24 12-pounders.

The *Dreadnought* gave its name to a class of battleship copied by other navies. Newly unified Germany, seeking to become a major sea power, built them. She also began building a craft whose destructive potential others had ignored—the U-boat or submarine, which was to be used in World War One.

The Kaiser's Germany

Kaiser Wilhelm II became ruler of the German Empire in 1888. He played an important part in her affairs.

Although Germany had a form of parliament, much domestic government, as well as the conduct of foreign affairs, was supposed to be left to the Kaiser.

The Kaiser's Germany, built on the foundations laid by Bismarck, prospered. It was a heavily industrialized country rich in natural resources. About half of its land was good for farming, while an abundance of coal and iron ore furnished raw materials for the two great industrial centres, the Ruhr and Silesia.

Germany was also rich in human resources. Most member states had first class education systems, and few of the people were illiterate. German skilled workers were among the finest, and soon Germany led the world in the production of chemicals and electrical products. It also produced more iron and steel than any other country in Europe. The standard of living rose and the population increased rapidly.

Meantime, Germany was flaunting her strength. Wilhelm increased the German Army and began building up the Imperial Navy to match Britain's Royal Navy. Germany also demanded colonies and obtained possessions in Africa and the East. As time went by Germany became more isolated from the other major powers.

Russia and France had become allies, and France and Britain had concluded the *Entente Cordiale*. In 1905 and 1911 Germany quarrelled with France over Morocco, and, on the second occasion, Wilhelm had to back down. In 1908 he accused Britain of rejecting Germany's friendship—and made people mistrust Germany even more. When Austria attacked Serbia in 1914, Wilhelm made last-ditch attempts to preserve peace. But his efforts were in vain, and for a generation he was blamed for the war.

▲ **Kaiser Wilhelm II with his wife, Augusta Victoria, and four of their sons.** Wilhelm was the grandson of Queen Victoria. He received a military education and had a passion for military splendour.

He fell out with his uncle, Edward VII, after the British king's visit to Berlin in 1909. Wilhelm described Edward as "a satan".

▲ **An example of German industrial efficiency: workers "clock in" at a factory.** The system meant that managers could ensure that their workers arrived on time.

▲ **An enormous hammer for beating steel** at the factory of the German weapons manufacturer, Alfred Krupp, at Essen.

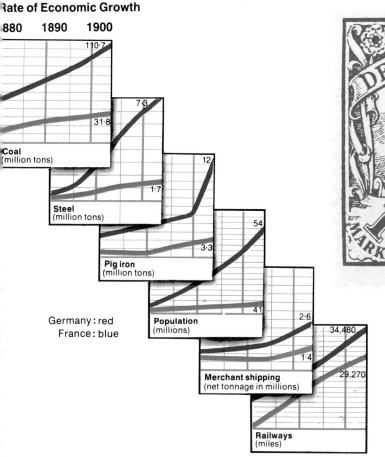

880   1890   1900

Coal
(million tons)

Steel
(million tons)

Pig iron
(million tons)

Population
(millions)

Merchant shipping
(net tonnage in millions)

Railways
(miles)

Germany: red
France: blue

110·7

31·8

7·3

1·7

12

3·3

54

41

2·6

1·4

34,480

29,270

▲ **Stamp from a German colony.** Jealousy of the other world powers caused Germany to acquire an overseas empire. But she failed to develop her new possessions. With Germany prospering, few people wanted to emigrate to the far-flung lands. Indeed, at one stage, Germany tried to sell South-West Africa to Britain.

◄ **This series of graphs clearly indicates the rise of Germany as an industrial nation at the end of the 19th century.** The comparison is with her arch-rival, France—for so long the leading power on the continent of Europe. Note the soaring population figures; they went on rising until 1914.

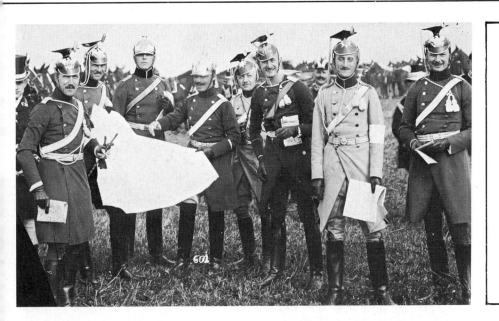

▲ **German officers on manoeuvres.** Wilhelm's love of the army encouraged traditional Prussian militarism. The privileged position of the German officer class in the German Empire meant that parliamentary government never really took root.

▲ **The "Captain of Köpenick"**; his practical joke revealed a deep respect for authority in Wilhelm's Germany.

The Captain of Köpenick

On 16 October, 1906, a shoemaker called Wilhelm Voigt dressed himself up as a Captain in the German Army and strode out into the streets of Berlin.

He encountered four soldiers, and immediately ordered them to follow him. So great was their respect for the authority of a captain's uniform that they obeyed instantly. The "captain" then picked up more troops in the same way. He led his band of followers to a railway station where they boarded a train bound for Köpenick, a small town outside Berlin.

When they arrived, the "captain" marched his troops to the town hall. They passed three policemen on the way, and these were duly ordered to fall in behind the "captain"—they too obeyed without question.

At the town hall, the "captain" demanded the sum of 4,002.50 marks to be paid to him. It was done, and the "captain" then ordered the arrest of the mayor of Köpenick. The mayor was taken off to the police station.

Altogether, Voigt's escapade lasted six hours before he was finally unmasked and arrested. He was sentenced to four years in prison, but his fame spread all over Europe. When he was released after two years, he went on a tour of Europe.

Alliances

During the late 19th and early 20th centuries,
the major European powers had formed a
complex network of alliances and under-
standings. These were designed to secure
peace and protection from aggression: in fact,
they meant that if one power were attacked,
all Europe could be drawn into the fray.

The broad result was that the two powers in
the centre of Europe, Germany and Austria–
Hungary, were surrounded by Britain, France
and Russia. Italy was in the curious position of
having agreements with both sides: she shared
the Triple Alliance (1882) with Germany and
Austria–Hungary, but she coveted some
Austro-Hungarian land.

▶ **The decaying Ottoman Empire remained aloof. Rumania was uncommitted and Serbia stood nominally alone.** But Serbia's smouldering quarrel with Austria–Hungary was a matter of much concern to Russia. The Russians and the Serbs were fellow Slavs, and Russia also had her own quarrel with Austria–Hungary; she wanted to be sure that Austria–Hungary did not expand eastwards.

47

GERMANY

Prague

BOHEMIA

MORAVIA

Cracow

GALICIA

RUSSIA

SLOVAKIA

Vienna

RUTHENIA

AUSTRIA

TYROL

Budapest

SLOVENIA

CROATIA

HUNGARY

RUMANIA

Belgrade

Bucharest

ITALY

BOSNIA

Sarajevo

HERZOGOVINA

SERBIA

BULGARIA

SANJAK OF NOVI PAZAR

Sofia

MONTENEGRO

Scutari

EASTERN RUMELIA

Constanti

MACEDONIA

Salonika

GREECE

TUR

Athens

- ▲ Czech
- ◨ Greek
- ◻ Slovene
- ▽ Slovak
- ◉ Romansh
- ▣ Rumanian
- △ Albanian
- ○ Croatian
- ▢ Osmanli (Turkish)
- △ Polish
- ▢ Tatar
- ▨ German
- ▨ Serbian
- ▣ Ruthenian (Ukrainian)
- ▢ Vlach
- ▲ Bulgarian
- ◍ Italian
- ▣ Magyar
- △ Macedonian Slav

▲ **The differing languages spoken by the inhabitants of Austria–Hungary and the Balkans.** The borders are those that existed before the Balkan Wars. The scattering of nationalities among the states was a source of unrest. Note the number of Serbs in Bosnia and Herzogovina, for example. It is easy to see why Serbia resented Austria–Hungary annexing these two states, and why "solutions" to the "Balkan Problem" always upset someone.

The Balkans in Turmoil

The Ottoman Empire, ruled by the Sultan of Turkey, was decaying. Turkey was nicknamed "the sick man of Europe".

In 1908, a group known as the Young Turks revolted and forced the Sultan to accept an elected parliament. Their activities set off a chain reaction in which most of the last Ottoman areas of Europe were lost. The Turkish collapse provoked a turbulence among many small nations in the Balkans, which was to reach its climax with the outbreak of World War One.

Several of the small Balkan states had been freed from the Ottoman Empire in the 19th century through the intervention of the major powers. Now the Austro–Hungarian Empire claimed two of the Ottoman provinces, Bosnia and Herzogovina. This provoked an international crisis.

Serbia had hoped to annex the two provinces, since many Serbs lived there. She protested strongly about the Ausrian claim. At one stage, war between Austria–Hungary and Serbia seemed likely, with the chance of the major powers becoming involved. It took diplomats of the big powers six months to find a peaceful solution.

It was in 1908 also that Bulgaria declared herself independent of the Ottoman Empire. Several of the Balkan nations wanted to annex the last remaining areas of the Ottoman Empire in Europe and in 1912-13, Serbia, Bulgaria, Greece, and Montenegro banded together and fought the Turks in the First Balkan War. The Turks were defeated and lost nearly all of their remaining territory in Europe, including Albania, which became independent, and Macedonia.

One of the victorious nations, Bulgaria, was dissatisfied with her share of the spoils. She declared war on Greece and Serbia in 1913 and the Second Balkan War began.

It lasted less than a month and Bulgaria was defeated, Rumania and the Turks attacking her as well as Serbia and Greece. Serbia emerged from these wars with twice as much territory as in 1912, and her Prime Minister, Nikola Pašić, said, "The first round is won. Now we must prepare for the second round—against Austria."

▲ **Franz Josef, Emperor of Austria–Hungary, at a family wedding.** In 1908, he had been on the throne for 60 years.

He ruled an Empire of 51 million people. They included Germans, Magyars, Poles, Czechs, Slovaks, Slovenes, Serbs, Croats, Ukrainians, Italians and Rumanians.

Austria–Hungary was, in fact, two kingdoms with two separate governments in Vienna and Budapest.

◀ **Serbian machine-gunners.** Serbia was a land-locked kingdom about the size of Scotland. After a revolt against the Turks in 1804, the Serbs had won the right to rule themselves; afterwards, they were always ready to help their fellow-Slavs in Bosnia and Herzogovina to win their freedom. But the great powers kept a wary eye on events in the Balkans.

In 1875-6, the Bosnians revolted and the great powers warned Serbia not to help them. The Congress of Berlin (1878) provided that Bosnia and Herzegovina be occupied by Austria–Hungary though they were to remain part of the Ottoman Empire.

After 1908, when Austria–Hungary annexed the two provinces, a secret society known as the Black Hand was formed to link Serbs in all countries. They plotted, ready for the day that they believed must come, when Serbia and Austria–Hungary would go to war.

The Main Events

The Boer War. Khaki-clad British infantrymen disembarking at Durban, South Africa.

British comment on the Russo–Japanese war: "Gallant little Jap" resisting Russian bear.

Russian workers on strike during the 1905 revolution in Russia.

1899
First Hague Conference fails to secure agreement on disarmament (May–July).
Marconi sends first wireless message across English Channel.
France: Dreyfus tried for the second time and again found guilty.
Magnetic tape-recorder invented by Valdemar Poulsen of Denmark.
Boer War starts 12 October. Battle of Elandslaagte won by British (21 October); British defeated at Nicholson's Nek (30 October); Battle of Modder River won by British (28 November); Buller's forces defeated at Colenso (15 December); Lord Roberts appointed British Commander-in-Chief, Lord Kitchener Chief of Staff (16 December).
Rudyard Kipling's *Stalky and Co.* published.
First large "luxury liner" launched, White Star Line's S.S. *Oceanic*.

1900
Boer War: Battle of Spion Kop, British defeated (24 January); Kimberley (15 February) and Ladysmith (28 February) relieved; British occupy Bloemfontein (March); British annex Orange Free State (24 May); British occupy Johannesburg (May); Mafeking relieved (17 May); British occupy Pretoria (June); British annex Transvaal (1 September); Boers turn to guerilla warfare.
Boxer Rising: Boxers besiege legations in Peking 20 June; legations relieved 14 August.
China declares war on big powers of Europe.
Britain: Circulation of *Daily Mail* reaches 1,000,000.
First trial flight of first zeppelin, LZ1, over Lake Constance, Germany.
King Humbert of Italy assassinated.
London's underground railways electrified.
Russians occupy Manchuria; 45,000 Chinese massacred.

1901
Victoria, Queen of England, dies (22 January); succeeded by Edward VII.
Boer War: Kitchener's offer of peace terms rejected by Boers.
President McKinley of United States assassinated (14 September); Theodore Roosevelt succeeds him.
Alberto Santos-Dumont flies around Eiffel Tower, Paris, in airship (19 October).
Empress Frederica of Germany dies (14 September).
Opening of Trans-Siberian Railway.
Toulouse-Lautrec dies.
Thomas Mann's *Buddenbrooks* published in Germany.
Rudyard Kipling's *Kim* published in Britain.
Strindberg's *The Dance of Death*.
Marconi sends wireless signals across Atlantic.
Nobel Prizes first awarded.
First electric tramcar runs in London.
First British submarine launched.
Commonwealth of Australia comes into being (1 January).

1902
Boer War ends with Treaty of Vereeniging (31 May).
Germany, Austria-Hungary, Italy renew Triple Alliance.
Secret treaty between France, Italy: Italy to remain neutral if France attacked.
Russo-Japanese agreement on Manchuria. Russians to evacuate territory for 18 months.
An Anglo-Japanese treaty signed.
King Edward VII of Britain crowned (9 August).
Trans-Siberian Railway reaches Vladivostok.
Trans-Pacific telegraph cable laid.
Immigration Restriction Act provides for a "white" Australia.
Enrico Caruso, Italian tenor, makes his first recording of *Vesti la Giubba*—first record to reach ultimate total sale of over a million.
Conan Doyle's *The Hound of the Baskervilles* published.
Première of Chekhov's *The Three Sisters*.

1903
Women's Social and Political Union formed in Britain to demand votes for women.
Wright brothers make first powered flights (17 December).
Ford Motor Company founded in United States.
First motor taxi-cabs in London.
Royal family of Serbia assassinated (11 June).
Wilhelm Einthoven invented electro-cardiograph.
Road speed limit in Britain raised to 20 m.p.h.
British expedition sent into Tibet.
Russia refuses to evacuate Manchuria as agreed with Japan in 1902.
Present-day Labour Party formed in Britain.
Premières of G. Bernard Shaw's *Man and Superman*.
The first story-film, *The Great Train Robbery*.
Pope Leo XIII dies; succeeded by Pope Pius X.
Gauguin dies.
United States lease canal zone from Panama.

1904
Entente Cordiale agreed between Britain, France.
Theodore Roosevelt elected President of United States (to 1909).
British expedition fights its way to Lhasa in Tibet.
Britain: Fisher becomes First Sea Lord.
Russo-Japanese War over Korea begins. Port Arthur besieged by Japanese by land and sea.
General strike in Italy.
Safety razor becomes popular; 12 million blades sold.
Construction of Panama Canal resumed.
Première of J. M. Barrie's *Peter Pan*.
Première of Chekhov's *The Cherry Orchard*.
Joseph Conrad's *Nostromo* published.
Picasso completes *The Two Sisters* painting.
Sir John Fleming invents thermionic valve for use in wireless sets.

1905
Sea Battle of Tsushima; Japanese annihilate Russian fleet (27 May).
Treaty of Portsmouth (New Hampshire) ends Russo-Japanese War; Russia defeated.
Revolution in Russia but Tsar Nicholas II's rule survives. "Bloody Sunday"—22 January. "October Manifesto" promises the formation of a parliament.
Italian protectorate established in Somaliland.
First Germany-France clash over Morocco begins.
Sinn Fein formed to support home rule for Ireland.
First real cinema opened at Pittsburg, U.S.A.
Wright brothers introduce "first practical aeroplane" *Flyer III*. Speed: 35 m.p.h. (56 k.p.h.).
Rising in German East Africa put down with some 75,000 Africans killed.
Baroness Orczy's *The Scarlet Pimpernel*, H. G. Wells's *Kipps* published.

1906
Highest court in France pronounces Dreyfus innocent.
Great Britain launches H.M.S. *Dreadnought*, "the ultimate battleship".
Conference at Algeciras provides solution to first Germany-France clash over Morocco.
Alberto Santos-Dumont makes first aeroplane flights in Europe, in France.
Annual average emigration of Germans drops from 750,000 (1870-1900) to 20,000.
Roald Amundsen, Norwegian explorer, completes voyage through North-West Passage (begun 1903).
Cézanne dies.
John Galsworthy's *The Man of Property*, first novel in the Forsyte Saga, published.
"Luxury liner" *Lusitania* launched.
San Francisco, U.S.A., suffers devastating earthquake.

1907
King Edward VII of Britain visits Tsar Nicholas II in
Russia.
Britain and Russia sign agreement of *Entente*.
Hague Peace Conference to limit armaments fails;
rejects ban on aerial bombing in war.
Mauretania crosses Atlantic at 26 knots.
William Willett proposes "daylight saving" in
Britain (adopted 1916).
Britain and Russia agree to stay out of Tibet.
British Parliament rejects plans for tunnel under
English Channel.
New Zealand becomes a Dominion.
Schoenberg's Chamber Symphony causes riot on
its first performance.
Première of J. M. Synge's *The Playboy of the
Western World*.
Electric washing-machine invented in the United
States.

1908
Young Turks revolt in Turkey; Sultan agrees to the
creation of a parliament.
Austria-Hungary annexes Bosnia and Herzegovina.
Bulgaria proclaims independence.
Henry Ford starts building Model T Ford ("Tin Lizzie").
Lord Baden-Powell starts the Boy Scouts.
Sir Ernest Shackleton leads expedition to within
100 miles of South Pole.
Britain: 75,000 watch F.A. Cup Final.
Kaiser Wilhelm II interview in *Daily Telegraph*
increases suspicion of Germany's intentions.
King Leopold II gives up Congo to Belgian state.
Wilbur Wright makes his first flights in Europe.
Kenneth Grahame's *The Wind in the Willows*
published.

**1909 advertisement for electric vacuum
cleaner,** as invented by Hubert Booth.

Girl revolutionary in Mexico. The revolution
begun in 1910 was not to end until 1916.
Venustiano Carranza emerged as victor.

1909
Russia, Bulgaria sign secret treaty against Germany,
Austria-Hungary.
Louis Bleriot flies English Channel by aeroplane in
37 minutes (25 July).
Henri Farman makes first 100-mile flight.
First labour exchanges opened in Britain.
Postal workers on strike in France.
Robert E. Peary, American explorer, becomes first
man to reach the North Pole.
Old age pensions introduced in Britain.
Diaghilev presents Russian ballet in Paris for first
time.
H. G. Wells's *Ann Veronica* published.
Premières of John Galsworthy's *The Silver Box,
Strife*.

1910
Edward VII, King of England dies (6 May); succeeded
by George V.
Strikes hit coal, shipping and wool industries in
Britain.
Union of South Africa becomes a Dominion.
Chinese armed expedition reaches Lhasa in Tibet.
Crippen arrested for murder on board ship as a result
of radio communication.
Zeppelin LZ4 starts world's first airline between
cities in Germany.
Revolution in Portugal; becomes a republic.
Louis Paulhan makes first aeroplane flight
London-Manchester for £10,000 prize.
Wassily Kandinsky finishes his first wholly abstract
painting.
First performance of Stravinsky's ballet, *The Firebird*.
Girl Guides started by Lady Baden-Powell.

1911
Italy invades Ottoman province of Libya.
British seamen and railway workers on strike.
Black Hand formed to "liberate all Serbs under
foreign domination".
Mona Lisa stolen from Louvre Museum, Paris.
(Recovered 1913.)
Second Germany-France clash over Morocco. Crisis
ends with Germany recognizing Morocco as French
protectorate.
Coronation of King George V in Britain.
Chinese Revolution. Sun Yat-sen elected President
of Southern China, 29 September.
Britain: Coal Mines Act prevents boys under 14 years
of age working below ground.
First performance of Stravinsky's ballet *Petrushka*.
Father Brown detective stories by G. K. Chesterton
published.
Amundsen becomes first man to reach South Pole.

1912
First Balkan War begins.
Albania proclaims independence.
Turkey cedes Libya to Italy.
Britain: miners and Port of London workers on strike.
Parliament promises miners minimum wage.
F. W. Woolworth opens his first chain store in
United States.
China: P'u Yi abdicates throne. Sun Yat-sen resigns.
Yuan Shih-K'ai elected provisional President in
China.
Britain: Royal Flying Corps formed.
Première of G. B. Shaw's *Pygmalion*.
Discovery in Britain of skull of Piltdown Man.
(Shown in 1953 to be a hoax.)

1913
First Balkan War ends.
Second Balkan War, June-August.
King George of Greece assassinated.
Special tax introduced in Germany to double strength
of army.
French increase compulsory military service for all
men from two years to three.
British suffragette, Emily Davison, runs on Derby
course, is killed.
First woman magistrate elected in Britain.
Old age and sickness insurance introduced in
United States, France, Germany.
Stravinsky's new ballet *The Rite of Spring* arouses
audience to fury.
D. H. Lawrence's *Sons and Lovers* published.
Charlie Chaplin's first film produced.
H. Geiger invents counter to measure radioactivity.
Harry Brearley produces stainless steel.

The Road to War, 1914
28 June. Assassination in Sarajevo.
5 July. Germany promises Austria-Hungary full
support against Serbia.
23 July. Austria-Hungary ultimatum to Serbia.
24 July. Russia decides to defend Serbia.
25 July. Serbian reply to ultimatum "unsatisfactory"
28 July. Austria-Hungary declares war on Serbia.
30 July. Russia calls up armies.
31 July. Germany warns Russia.
1 August. Germany declares war on Russia.
3 August. Germany declares war on France.
4 August. Germany invades Belgium. Great Britain
declares war on Germany.
6 August. Austria-Hungary declares war on Russia.
Serbia declares war on Germany.

Bernhardt, Sarah (1844-1923), whose real name was Henriette Rosine Bernard, was the greatest actress of her day. She was born in Paris and achieved her first great success in 1869. Soon, the critics were lavish in their praise of her. She toured all over the world and founded her own Théâtre Sarah Bernhardt in Paris in 1899. In 1915, her right leg had to be amputated but she was not deterred. She went on to tour America in 1917 and created her last role in 1922.

Blériot, Louis (1872-1936), the French aviation pioneer, made the first overseas aeroplane flight when he crossed the English Channel on 25 July, 1909. He took off from Baraques at 4.40 a.m. and landed at 5.17 a.m. in a field near Dover to win a *Daily Mail* prize of £1,000. He went on to build aircraft for the French government during World War One.

Curie, Marie (1867-1934) was born Marja Sklodowska in Poland and left home to study in Paris. She married Pierre Curie and together they began work to find out about radio-active materials. They obtained eight tons of pitchblende and, for four years, tried to isolate the radio-active material in it. In the end, they produced a teaspoonful of a new radio-active metal, and they named it radium. Their work was to be invaluable in the development of X-rays. When Pierre was killed in a street accident in 1906, Marie was given his job as a professor in the University of Paris.

Diaghilev, Sergei Pavlovich (1872-1929). Russian ballet producer, company director and impresario. Diaghilev may be credited with the rescue of ballet from the tinsel spectacle it had become by the end of the 19th century. His originality and flair effected a particularly important dance revolution in the West, where ballets such as *Petrushka* (Stravinsky), *Scheherazade* (Rimsky-Korsakov) and *L'Apres Midi d'un Faune* (Debussy), created a sensation and remain part of contemporary repertoire. His two great dancers were Anna Pavlova and Vaslav Nijinsky.

Dreyfus, Alfred (1859-1935). French soldier and cause of a French national crisis. The young officer was wrongly accused and convicted of passing information to the Germans. The Dreyfus case dragged on for twelve years, from 1894-1906. It exposed deep anti-Jewish feeling in high places, and the terrible rigidity of French government and army officials, who could not "afford" to admit their mistake. It was also responsible for *J'accuse*, an article by the great novelist Emile Zola—a landmark in the history of journalism.

Edison, Thomas Alva (1847-1931) started his career as a telegraph operator. In 1870, he invented a machine for printing telegraph messages on a strip of paper tape and later set up a scientific workshop at New Jersey. He invented the gramophone, the electric lamp, the kinetoscope or peepshow for viewing small moving pictures, and a moving picture camera. Altogether, his inventions totalled 1,097.

Edward VII, King of England (1841-1910) reigned from 1901. He was a popular figure, nicknamed "Tum-Tum", who mingled freely with people of fashion. He loved sport, eating, and the company of beautiful women. He often travelled abroad and was the first British monarch to visit Russia, which he did in 1907. He showed great interest in foreign affairs, and his personal influence in the *Entente Cordiale* with France was considerable.

Ford, Henry (1836-1947) built his first motor car in the United States in 1896. In 1903 he founded the Ford Motor Company and at first built cars which only the rich could afford. Then, in 1908, he decided to bring down the price by building only one type of car—the Model T. nicknamed the "Tin Lizzie". It was the first

car cheap enough for large numbers of people to buy, and, over the next 20 years, over 15 million were to be sold.

Ford pioneered mass production methods and it was he who introduced the assembly line. Although it brought great benefits to the public, mass production involved many workers in work that was monotonous; they often did the same small job repeatedly, day in, day out. Few could take a craftsman's pride in his work.

David Lloyd George, British politician.

George, David Lloyd (1863-1945) was a fiery Welshman who began his career as a solicitor. As Chancellor of the Exchequer in Britain from 1908-1915, he introduced old age pensions and national health insurance. He was a Non-conformist, and considered very radical at the turn of the century; apart from his social reforms, he was pro-Boer during the Boer War, believing that Britain was acting aggressively toward a smaller nation. He was Member of Parliament for Caernarvon for 55 years, having first been elected in 1890. He became Prime Minister during World War One, in 1916.

Giolitti, Giovanni (1842-1928) was Prime Minister of Italy no less than five times between 1892 and 1921. He introduced some social and agrarian reforms and extended the franchise in Italy, but in using strong measures to suppress strikes, he lost the support of Italian Socialists. Although opposed to colonial adventures, he was responsible for Italy's invasion of Libya. On the outbreak of World War One, he tried to keep Italy neutral but she entered the conflict on the side of the Allies in 1915.

Jaurès, Jean (1859-1914) had, by 1914, become the acknowledged leader of French Socialism. He entered the French Chamber of Deputies in 1885. Although many French socialists felt that the Dreyfus Case was a distraction from the struggle of the working class, Jaurès brought many to feel, like him, that Dreyfus' innonence must be defended. He helped to create a single French socialist party in 1905. He was assassinated shortly after war broke out in 1914.

Franz Josef I (1830-1916), Emperor of Austria from 1848, King of Hungary from 1867. At the turn of the century, Franz Josef was an aged monarch ruling over the great empire of Austria-Hungary. He had begun his reign as an autocrat, but had been forced to modify his manner because of the attitude of his subject peoples, many of whom had nationalist aims. The assassination of his heir, the Archduke Franz Ferdinand, by Serbian nationalists started off a chain of events that ended in World War One.

Kruger, Stephanus Johannes Paulus (1825-1904) took part, as a boy, in the Great Trek made by the Boers from Cape Colony to the Transvaal in 1835-7. In 1883 he was appointed president of the Transvaal and again in 1888, 1893, and 1898. Nicknamed *Oom Paul* (Uncle Paul), he led the Boers at the outbreak of the Boer War. He died in exile in Switzerland.

Marconi, Guglielmo (1874-1937), the Italian inventor passed the first wireless signal in history between two rooms in his home. He was 20 at the time, and two years later he was sending messages in Morse code over a distance of two miles. No one in Italy was interested in his invention, so he went to London to develop it. In 1901 he passed a signal across the Atlantic Ocean.

Meiji Tenno (Mutsuhito) (1852-1912) was Emperor of Japan from 1867. On his accession to the throne, Japan was still organized on medieval lines; local barons played a prominent part in the affairs of the people and an official called the *shogun* ruled for the emperor. Meiji took back his right to rule and put down a rebellion of the *shogun's* supporters. Afterwards, he became the central figure in the movement to "westernize" Japan.

Nicholas II (1868-1918) was Tsar of Russia from 1894 to 1917. He ruled over a vast empire, most of whose inhabitants were peasants. Dissatisfaction with the Tsar's autocratic rule came to a head in the revolution of 1905. After this, Nicholas introduced a *Duma*, a form of parliament but with less power than the revolutionaries had hoped for. A kindly man, he lacked the strength of will to control the forces of change in Russia and he came increasingly under the control of his wife and her sinister confidant, the monk Rasputin.

Pankhurst, Mrs Emmeline (1858-1928) was born Emmeline Goulden and married Dr Richard Pankhurst in 1879. She became leader of the British suffragettes, organizing the Womens' Social and Political Union in 1903. Imprisoned and force-fed, she remained a staunch patriot and in 1914 she called on suffragettes to end their campaigning and help Britain win the war. She was to die on the day when Parliament finally granted the vote to all women over the age of 21.

Meiji Tenno, Emperor of Japan.

Theodore Roosevelt, American President.

Sun Yat-sen (1866-1923) fled from China in 1895 after leading an unsuccessful rising against the Emperor. He plotted ten more risings from abroad and was finally successful in the revolution of 1911. He became President of Southern China on its liberation. When the Emperor was driven out in the North, Sun resigned to allow the victorious Yuan Shih-k'ai to be President of the whole of China. But Yuan made himself a dictator and Sun led a revolt against him. It was unsuccessful, and Sun was once again forced to flee the country.

Wilhelm II (1859-1941) was Kaiser of the German Empire from 1888-1918. Though he ruled with a form of parliament, he was responsible for most of Germany's policies. After sacking Bismarck, the "Iron Chancellor", he personally supervised the build-up of Germany's military and naval strength.

Wright, Wilbur (1867-1912) and Orville (1871-1948) began work as bicycle-makers in Dayton, Ohio. At the same time, they made a thorough study of all the available literature on attempts to fly in a heavier-than-air craft. They built three biplane gliders which they test-flew on the sand dunes at Kitty Hawk, North Carolina. With the third glider, they made more than one thousand flights, and in their fourth they put a light-weight petrol engine. In this machine, which they called *Flyer*, they made the first successful aeroplane flight.

Zapata, Emiliano (1883-1919) was a leader in the Mexican Revolution of 1910-16. Born in a small town in the south of Mexico, Zapata raised an army there to fight for land for the people. At one stage he joined forces with the bandit leader, Pancho Villa, and in 1914 they occupied Mexico City.

Picasso, Pablo (1881-1973). The originator of *Cubism* in Modern Art. A Spaniard by birth, he developed his art in France, where he became one of the "new art's" leading lights. Picasso and another artist, Georges Braque, together worked out the theory of Cubism between 1906 and 1910, in a series of *montages* (a combination of painting, drawing, and bits of paper, wood and other objects glued to the canvas). Until 1918, his paintings were mainly abstract; he attempted to create his own forms, not to imitate nature. Afterwards, his style changed many times, but his influence on Modern Art remained consistent and strong.

Rasputin, Gregory Efimovitch (1871-1916) was born a poor peasant in Siberia and became a monk in an obscure religious sect. In 1907, he was introduced to Tsar Nicholas and the Tsarina and attempted to cure their son of haemophilia by faith healing. He appeared to be successful and afterwards exerted power over the Tsar and Tsarina. He was soon widely hated and feared. A group of noblemen assassinated him in 1916.

Roberts, Frederick (1832-1914). British soldier. His successful campaigns in India and Afghanistan earned him the Victoria Cross, a K.C.B. and G.C.B., and in 1892 he was created Baron Roberts of Kandahar and Waterford. He was sent out as Commander-in-Chief of the Army in South Africa in January 1900, after numerous British defeats there. He captured in turn Kimberley, Bloemfontein and Pretoria, after which he handed over his command to Lord Kitchener. He was created Commander-in-Chief of the British Army, and is buried in St. Paul's Cathedral.

Roosevelt, Theodore (1858-1919) was Vice President when President William McKinley was assassinated in 1901. When he succeeded to the presidency, he was the youngest President of the United States, at 42 years of age. He was elected to serve a full term in 1904. "Teddy" Roosevelt was a popular figure. He enjoyed outdoor sports, and had conquered his asthma as a child by vigorous physical activity. He led a cavalry regiment in the Spanish-American War (1899) and as President determined to make America a strong international power. "Teddy bears" are named after him, dating from a time when a cartoonist showed him with a bear-cub.

Faces of the Future

Albert Einstein published his theory of relativity in 1905 and became famous.

Sigmund Freud. In 1900, *The Interpretation of Dreams* made people aware of psychology.

Mohandas K. Gandhi was a solicitor in South Africa at the turn of the century.

Benito Mussolini, a blacksmith's son, was editor of the socialist newspaper *Avanti!*

Nations and Empires

Imperialism is the desire to acquire or extend an empire. Nationalism is the feeling of loyalty to a nation or race. Both affected international affairs, but in different ways.

▲ **British maxim-gun detachment in India.** In the last analysis, the preservation of empires and frontiers in the pre-1914 world often depended on military strength. Limited wars were still possible.

▼ **A cruel British cartoon of an Irishman supporting Home Rule for Ireland.** The demand for freedom from British rule was given a focus by the formation of the *Sinn Fein* (Ourselves Alone) party in 1905.

The British Empire had become the greatest Empire that the world had ever known; the Empire on which, it was said, the sun never set. It girdled the globe from the Dominion of Canada to the continent of Australia, including large portions of Africa and the sub-continent of India. At its heart was a thriving industrial nation and watching over its maritime trade was the most powerful navy in the world.

At the other end of the scale was the decaying Ottoman Empire, headed, until 1908, by a corrupt autocrat who did not accept the need for progress in industry and agriculture.

In between, there were empires a varying stages of development. Ther was the massive sprawl of Russia acros two continents, taking in one sixth of the land surface of the globe, a vast empir with a doomed emperor. There was th emerging empire of newly-unified Ger many—a symbol of that nation's grow ing strength.

Nationalism had united Germany in the 19th century, and also brought to gether the isolated kingdoms of Italy But inside the Austro–Hungarian and Ottoman Empires it had the revers effect, breaking up empires as smal national groups struggled for independ ence. Poles wanted freedom from Rus sia; the Irish, independence from Britain

In China, nationalism took the form of protest against the ineffective rule o the Manchus. This led to rebellion in 1911, and afterwards China became a republic. The Young Turks of the Otto man Empire were nationalists who over threw the Sultan. Nationalists of thi sort were alive to the need for thei country to make progress on wester lines in a rapidly changing world.

▲ **China, 1911.** A revolutionary soldier cuts off a peasant's pigtail. The pigtail was looked on as a symbol of the old order, and China was at last marching into the modern world.

▲ **Macedonian revolutionaries, 1903.** Macedonia was the last large area of Europe under the direct rule of the Ottoman Empire. Peopled by a variety of races, it was coveted by both Greece and Bulgaria.

Two groups of Macedonian rebels emerged, one working for union with Bulgaria and the other striving for independence. Greece sent troops to root out these rebels because she had her own interest in Macedonia.

▲ **Italian artillery in action in Libya.** Newly unified Italy had imperial ambitions. In the 19th century, she had acquired two hot, disease-ridden territories in East Africa—Eritrea and Somaliland. Then she tried to invade Ethiopia and suffered a humiliating defeat. In October 1911, Italy invaded the Ottoman province of Libya in North Africa. By September 1912, the conquest was complete. Turkey ceded Libya to Italy.

The outcome of the revolution was complex. Southern China at once became a republic under Sun Yat-sen but the Manchu emperor, a six-year-old boy, kept control in the north. He was driven out by Yuan Shih-k'ai, and Sun stepped down to allow Yuan to lead all China. When Yuan acted as a dictator, Sun led an unsuccessful revolt. Many years of struggle lay ahead for Sun and his *Kuomintang* (Nationalist Party).

The Young Turks

As the Ottoman Empire crumbled during the 19th century, a nationalist group called the Young Turks emerged. They hoped to revive Turkey. The Sultan, Abdul Hamid II, ruled without a parliament and the Young Turks believed that a parliament was essential to the fulfilment of their hopes.

In July 1908, they led a revolt of the Turkish Third Army in Macedonia and their example was followed by troops elsewhere. A general sent to quell the revolt was shot dead.

The Young Turk leaders sent a telegram to the Sultan outlining what they wanted. He gave in and agreed to stop ruling as an autocrat; Turkey would have a parliament. When the news was announced, there was rejoicing in the streets throughout the kingdom.

Elections took place in 1909 and Young Turks won seats in the new parliament. In time, three of them controlled the government—Enver, Talat and Djemal. They improved social conditions, extended education and tried to change old-fashioned Muslim ideas. But they failed to solve the problems of an empire containing so many different racial and religious groups.

◀ **Young Turk rosettes on sale in Turkey after the 1908 revolution.** Note the fezes and the veiled women; Muslims had a prominent place in Turkish society. In 1909, some rioted in Constantinople against the Young Turks.

Writers and Dramatists

▲ *Ubu Roi* **(King Ubu) in a modern production of Alfred Jarry's startling play.**

Ubu Roi was first produced in Paris in 1896. It opened with a single four-letter word and at once fighting broke out in the audience between supporters of Jarry and his opponents. It was 15 minutes before the play was resumed. Jarry used the wildest absurdities to ridicule the comfortable values of the middle classes. He introduced a new type of drama—the theatre of the absurd. Jarry himself was a bohemian character and drank himself to death at an early age.

▲ **Scene from Chekhov's** *The Three Sisters* **of 1901.** His plays have an atmosphere of wistful humour and pathos. The characters, like those in his many short stories, are ordinary people rather than heroes or villains.

▶ **Scene from Shaw's** *The Doctor's Dilemma* **in a production in 1906.** In all of his plays, Shaw attempted to drive home a message rather than to examine character or emotion. In this play he attacked the medical profession.

In the early years of the 20th century, literature, like the other arts, entered into a period of change.

In the 19th century, great writers like Dickens, Balzac and Tolstoy had presented broad views of society, packed with detail, social comment and excitement. Their novels appealed both to the highly-educated, and to ordinary people who simply wanted a good story.

By 1900, fewer novelists were producing works which were considered both "artistic" and popular bestsellers. It was said in Britain that "Conrad and Hardy seem likely to be the last novelists of repute known to the general public."

Two of the greatest novelists of the 20th century, Proust and Joyce, were appreciated only by a select few. They did describe the society in which they lived—Proust, for example, was fascinated by innovations like the telephone and motor car—but their novels required very careful reading. Others, like Thomas Mann and André Gide, kept to a style that was easier to understand, but their novels did not contain the exciting plots, the drama and sensation that the new reading public demanded.

In contrast, the period saw a great boom in popular publishing, for universal education had created a vast new market. Many best-sellers were destined to survive and are still read avidly today. Conan Doyle had already created a taste for detective stories and when he killed off Sherlock Holmes the public demanded his return. Doyle relented and raised his hero from the dead in 1903.

Edgar Wallace wrote his first mystery story in 1905 and Baroness Orczy's *The Scarlet Pimpernel* came out in the same year. At the same time, H. G. Wells was achieving a mammoth output of science fiction and social novels.

Social problems were at the heart of much of the theatre of the day. The role of women in society had been treated by Ibsen, and the theme was taken up by George Bernard Shaw. Shaw wrote eight major plays between 1900 and 1914; all had a strong social or political message. The tormented Swedish dramatist August Strindberg examined the institution of marriage in *The Dance of Death* (1901).

Anton Chekhov was another giant of the theatre. He described the situation of the privileged classes in Russia, bewildered by the rumbling forces of social change that were launching Russia into the modern world.

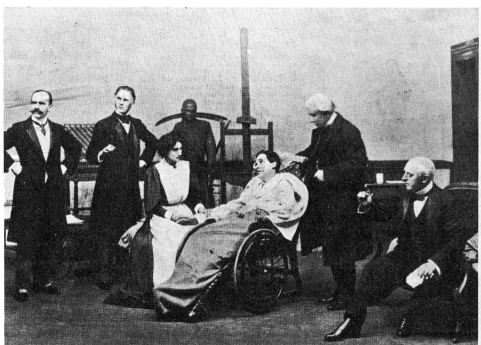

▲ Anton Chekhov regarded himself as a social chronicler of his times. He was born in Taganrog in Russia and worked as a doctor until 1886 when his first book, *Motley Stories,* proved a success.

After that he concentrated on writing, although he helped in a cholera epidemic in 1892-3. His plays, *The Seagull, Uncle Vanya, The Three Sisters* and *The Cherry Orchard* were written between 1896 and his death in 1904.

▲ Thomas Mann, probably the greatest modern German novelist. He wrote his first short stories while working as an insurance clerk in Munich. The first was published when he was 19 years old.

Mann became famous with the appearance of his first novel, *Buddenbrooks,* in 1901. *Tonio Kröger* (1903) and *Death in Venice* (1912) added to his reputation, but his best work was to come after World War One.

▲ André Gide, French poet, novelist, essayist and critic. He was the son of a wealthy family and was able to devote all his time to writing. His first book, *The Notebooks of André Walter* (1891), was followed by a succession of works in which he repeatedly changed his style.

He lived in Paris and had a great influence on the literature of his time, both through personal contact and the *Nouvelle Revue Française* which he founded in 1909.

▲ An illustration from H. G. Wells's *The First Men in the Moon* (1901), in which he anticipated some of the problems which would arise from the comparative lack of gravity on the moon. In addition to science fiction, Wells wrote social and comic novels such as *Kipps* (1905) and *The History of Mr Polly* (1910).

◄ An illustration from Arthur Conan Doyle's *The Hound of the Baskervilles* (1902). Conan Doyle trained as a doctor and published his first book featuring Sherlock Holmes, in 1887. Conan Doyle's novels of crime and mystery were so popular that many other writers began to produce books in the same genre.

Steam Turbine

Materials

2 5″ square sheets of cooking foil
Thin card, approx 5″ square (as
from a cornflake packet)
Contact adhesive
Pencil
A pair of compasses
Small hand drill, with 2.5 mm. ($\frac{1}{8}$″)
drill bit and 5 mm. ($\frac{1}{4}$″) drill bit
*A tin can with lid (as for drinking
chocolate), approx 4″ long, 2$\frac{3}{4}$″ dia.
3 washers
2 nuts
2ba bolt, 4 cm. (1$\frac{1}{2}$″) long
Water
Bunsen burner (or similar stove)
*If a larger tin is used, the holes must
be at the same centres as shown in
the diagram.

The turn of the century was the great age of steam. This project shows you how to make a model that will demonstrate the principle of the steam turbine.

Step 1. Spread a thin film of adhesive onto one side of the cooking foil and one side of the card and allow to dry. When dry, carefully lay the glued side of the card over the foil and press the two surfaces together.

Repeat for the other side of the card, using the second piece of foil. The foil will protect the card from warping when it is exposed to the steam.

Step 2. Carefully mark out the foil-covered card, as shown in figure 1. The lines should be pencilled in lightly to avoid damaging the foil.

Begin by drawing a 1 inch diameter circle. Then draw a 4 inch diameter circle from the same centre.

Make a mark "A" on the outer circle. Mark off point "B" with the compasses set as for the 4 inch circle, using A as the centre.

Repeat around the outer circle until you come back to point A. Join A to D, B to E, C to F. Each of these lines shoul[d] pass through the centre.

Next, bisect A–B by making two arc[s] of the same radius, one from point A an[d] one from point B. From the point a[t] which the arcs cross, draw a line throug[h] the centre of the circle. This gives yo[u] points G and K. Beginning at K, mar[k] off H, L, J, and F in the same way as yo[u] did for A, B, C etc.

Step 3. From the centre of the circl[e] draw a small circle of the same diamete[r] as the outside of one of the washers. Dri[ll] a $\frac{1}{4}$ inch diameter hole through the cen-tre of the circle. Glue the washer ove[r] the hole so that it fits the small circle.

Carefully cut along all of the dotte[d] lines. Twist each of the 12 blades so tha[t] the fan looks like the one in figure 2[.] This is best done by laying the fan on [a] flat surface with the washer side down[.] Then press down on the centre of th[e] fan with one hand, while twisting th[e] blades with the other hand.

Figure 1
Marking out the turbine fan

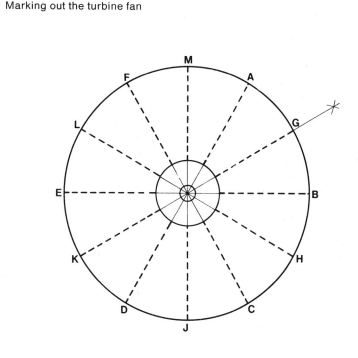

Figure 2
The completed fan

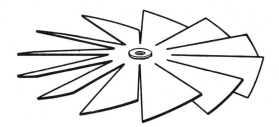

tep 4. Drill two $\frac{1}{8}$ inch diameter holes pposite one another through the rim of he tin (see figure 3). These holes will orm jets for the steam to pass through.

Drill a $\frac{1}{4}$ inch hole through the centre f the tin lid. (It may be necessary to put foot on the lid while you are drilling, a order to stop it from revolving.) Put he screw through the hole so that the crew is pointing out of the tin. Tighten he nuts and ensure that the screw is at ight angles to the tin lid.

Operation. Put about a cupful of water a the tin, so that the tin is about a third ull. Fit on the lid, making sure that it eals properly. Fit the turbine fan over he screw with the washer side down-vards: the fan should then rotate freely n the screw. If the fan tends to hang ower on one side, trim away a small trip from the lowest blade until the fan balances. Make sure the fan rotates reely without touching the tin.

Place the assembly on a tripod over a Bunsen burner and adjust the flame to about a quarter of its full pressure. Make sure that the flame does not rise above the base of the tin. (The assembly an be placed on a gas cooker, but take are that it is well balanced.)

Stand back and wait for the water to boil (this will take a couple of minutes). When steam begins to escape from the holes in the rim of the tin, it will cause he turbine to rotate in the same way as the wind makes a windmill turn. You an give the turbine a start, but this is not usually necessary if it revolves freely.

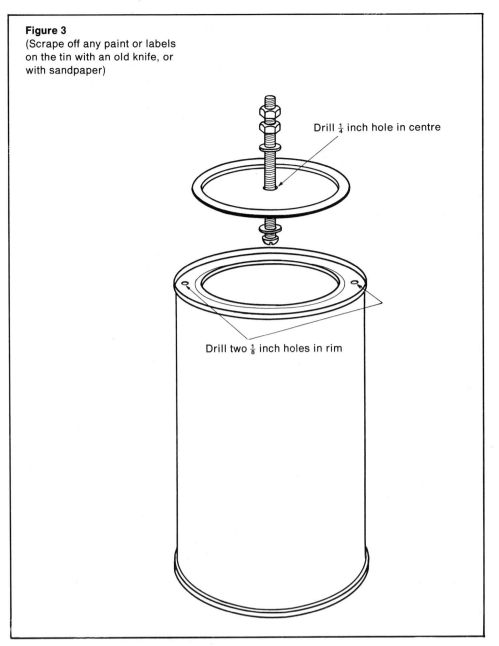

Figure 3
(Scrape off any paint or labels on the tin with an old knife, or with sandpaper)

Drill $\frac{1}{4}$ inch hole in centre

Drill two $\frac{1}{8}$ inch holes in rim

Points to watch. Do not touch the tin or blades with the hands! Steam and boiling water can give bad burns.

Do not turn the gas up too high: boiling water may escape from the jets. It is best to start with a low flame and increase it gradually until the best working pressure is found.

Do not operate for more than five minutes in case the water boils dry.

When you have finished using the apparatus, allow plenty of time for it to cool down before removing it.

Steam power. In a full size steam turbine, several fans of up to 12 feet in diameter are mounted on a shaft. This shaft drives the electricity generator or other machinery. Steam under a very high pressure is piped to the turbine and this causes the blades to rotate at very high speeds providing thousands of horse-power. You can find more information on steam turbines in your local library.

The Wright Brothers' Aircraft

Materials
Balsa wood 4″ x 2″ x 3/32″
Balsa wood 3/32″ x 3/16″ — 9 ft (A)
Balsa wood 1/16″ x 1/16″ — 3 ft (B)
Stiff card 14″ x 11″
Graph paper with ¼″ squares,
14″ × 11″ light coloured or white
Tube of balsa cement
Small modelling knife
Eyebrow tweezers
Black cotton
Tissue paper and fine glass paper

Step 1 Copy the three views of the aircraft onto the graph paper, using the squares to plot points. Make sure that this is done with the greatest possible accuracy. Use ink or soft pencil to ensure that the drawing stands out well on the squared paper. The areas shown in solid black will have balsa sections glued on to them.

Print the lettering in ink, and then mount the sheet on the card, using a good paper adhesive.

Step 2: The Plan View Cut the two rudder sections from balsa A and glue them to the plan. Use the eyebrow tweezers to assist the handling of small parts. Cut the 37 wing ribs from balsa A, shaping them as shown with a knife and glass paper. Glue them to the plan. Repeat the process for the elevator, using 9 ribs; you will need to reduce the thickness of these to $\frac{1}{8}$ in with glass paper.

Make up the two wing-tips from sections of balsa A laid flat. Glue on sections of balsa B for the remaining parts shown in black. Fix lengths of cotton along the dotted lines; these are the bracing wires (Figure 1).

Technical drawings of aircraft often show the three main views; the front, side and plan views. This project shows how to build 3-dimensional "pictures" of aircraft, using each view as the basis for a picture. It is based on the Wrights' Flyer I.

Step 3: the Front Elevation Cut 9 lengths of balsa B for the wing struts (see Figure 2). Glue them in place, then attach the cotton along the dotted lines for the bracing wires.

Cut two lengths of balsa A for the main wings. Sand down the leading edges and glue the main wings in place.

Cut and sand the elevator from balsa A and assemble as shown in Figure 2. All of the struts are cut from balsa B. Glue the structure to points X and Y, and to the drawing at Z.

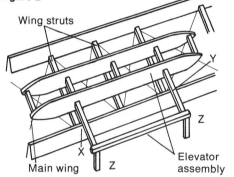

Figure 2

Wing struts
Main wing
X
Y
Z
Z
Elevator assembly

Step 4: the Side Elevation Cut the frames and struts that are to be laid flat against the drawing from balsa B. Glue them to the drawing. To make the wings and elevator cut the sheet balsa out as shown in Figure 3 and then cover the underside of each wing with

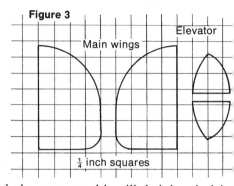

Figure 3

Main wings
Elevator
¼ inch squares

balsa cement; this will shrink as it dries and make the wing curve.

Glue the wings in place on the drawing; the main wings should slope downwards slightly, as may be seen on the drawing of the Front Elevation. Make the propellor from balsa A, and round off the edges of a length of balsa B to make the shaft and the mounting struts.

Cut wing struts and attach them to the wings and elevator as shown. Glue two strips of balsa A on the frame to form the rudder. Fix the cotton bracing wires as shown (Figure 4).

Finishing Cut pieces of tissue paper slightly larger than the wing and elevator on the plan view and glue them onto the balsa. When dry, the edges of the tissue may be cut to size with the modelling knife. You can make the balsa look more like the original spruce by giving it two or three coats of varnish

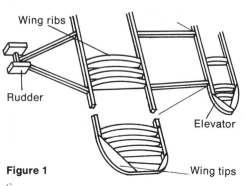

Wing ribs
Rudder
Elevator
Wing tips

Figure 1

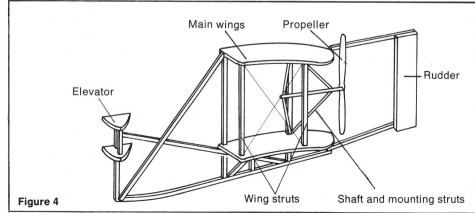

Main wings
Propeller
Elevator
Rudder
Wing struts
Shaft and mounting struts

Figure 4

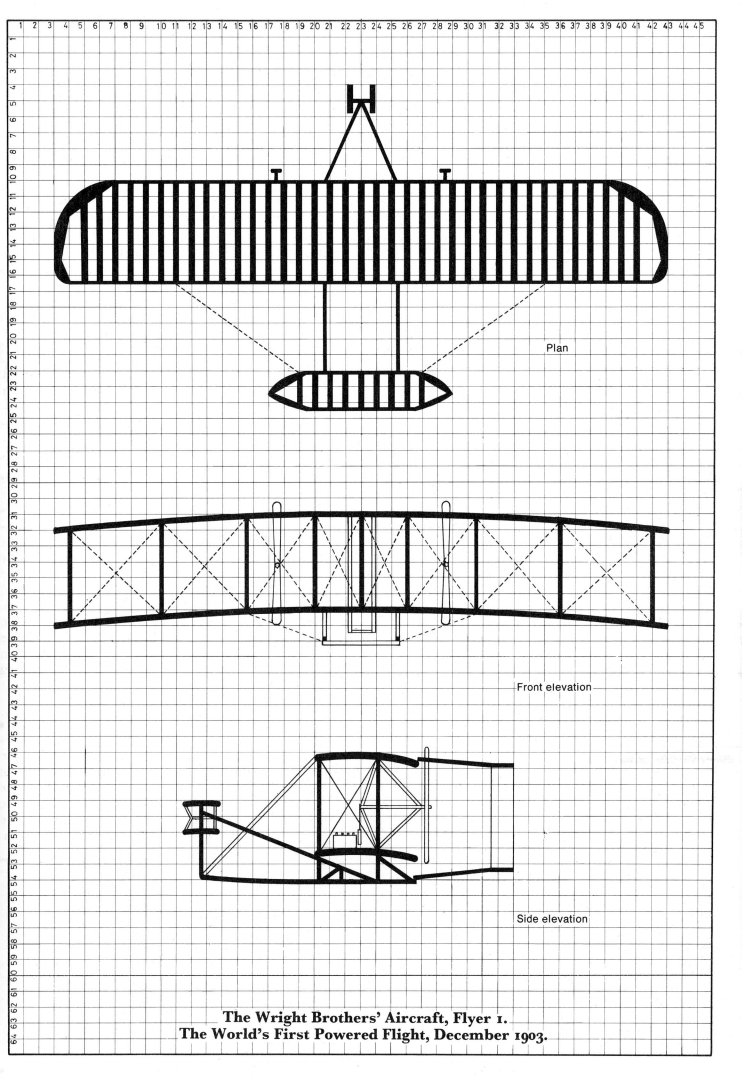

Plan

Front elevation

Side elevation

**The Wright Brothers' Aircraft, Flyer 1.
The World's First Powered Flight, December 1903.**

Index

Further Reading

Available in the United States and Canada:

ALLEN, FREDERICK LEWIS. *Great Pierpont Morgan.* Harper & Row 1949.
BAILEY, THOMAS A. *A Diplomatic History of the American People.* Appleton-Century-Crofts 1969.
BEALE, HOWARD KENNEDY. *Theodore Roosevelt and the Rise of the America to World Power.* Macmillan 1966.
BLUM, JOHN MORTON. *Republican Roosevelt.* Harvard University Press 1954.
DULLES, FOSTER RHEA. *Labor In America.* Crowell 1961.
FAULKNER, HAROLD U. *The Quest for Social Justice, 1898-1914.* (History of Life Series), Watts 1971.
GLAD, PAUL W. *The Trumpet Soundeth: William Jennings Bryan and His Democracy, 1896-1912.* University of Nebraska Press 1960.
HANDLIN, OSCAR. *The Uprooted.* Atlantic Monthly Press 1973.
HANSEN, MARCUS L. *Immigrant In America.* Harper & Row 1969.
HERNDON, BOOTON. *Ford: An Unconventional Biography of the Men and Their Times.* Weybright 1969.
JOSEPHSON, MATTHEW. *The Robber Barons.* Harcourt, Brace Jonavoich 1934.
Life History of the United States, Vol. 8, 1890-1901. Time 1964.
Life History of the United States, Vol. 9, 1901-1917. Time 1964.
LINK, ARTHUR S. *Woodrow Wilson: A Brief Biography.* Watts 1972.
MOWRY, GEORGE E. *Era of Theodore Roosevelt, 1900-1912.* Harper & Row 1958.
O'NEILL, WILLIAM L., ed. *Echoes of Revolt: The Masses, 1911-1917.* Quadrangle Books 1966.
REGIER, C. C. *Era of the Muckrakers.* University of North Carolina Press 1932.
RIIS, JACOB A. *How the Other Half Lives.* Peter Smith 1959.
STEFFENS, LINCOLN. *The Shame of the Cities.* Peter Smith 1959.
This Fabulous Century, Vol. I, 1900-1910. Time 1969.
This Fabulous Century, Vol. II, 1910-1920. Time 1964.
WECTER, DIXON. *Saga of American Society.* Scribners 1970.
WITTKE, CARL. *We, Who Built America; The Saga of the Immigrant.* Prentice-Hall 1967.

Available in Britain:

BORER, MARY CATHCART. *Britain—Twentieth Century.* Warne 1966.
BORER, MARY CATHCART. *The Boer War: 10 October 1899-31 May 1902.* Lutterworth Press 1971.
BUCK, PEARL. *The Man who Changed China (Sun Yat-sen).* Methuen 1955.
CECIL, ROBERT. *Life in Edwardian England.* Batsford 1969.
CHAMPION, HAROLD. *The True Book about Emmeline Pankhurst.* Muller 1963.
DOORLY, ELEANOR. *The Radium Woman (Madame Curie).* Heinemann, 1939.
FLEMING, D. F. *The Origins and Legacies of World War One.* Allen & Unwin, 196
GLINES, CARROLL V. *The Wright Brothers: Pioneers of Power Flight.* Watts 196
GORDON, SYDNEY. *Thomas Alva Edison.* Blackwell 1966.
JOHN, DAVID (compiler). *The Anglo-Boer War.* Jackdaw Publications 1969.
JULLIAN, PHILIPPE. *Edward and the Edwardians.* Sidgwick & Jackson 1967.
KAZANTZIS, JUDITH (editor). *Women in Revolt: The Fight for Emancipation.* Jackdaw Publications 1967.
KESTEVEN, G. R. *The Boer War.* Chatto & Windus 1971.
LAMBERT, RICHARD S. *The Twentieth Century: Britain, Canada, U.S.A.* Grant 1963.
LINECAR, HOWARD. *Early Aeroplanes.* Benn 1965.
MINNEY, R. J. *The Edwardian Age.* Cassell 1964.
NICKELS, S. (editor). *Assassination at Sarajevo.* Jackdaw Publications 1966.
NOWELL-SMITH, SIMON (editor). *Edwardian England, 1901-1914.* Oxford University Press 1964.
PETRIE, SIR CHARLES. *Scenes of Edwardian Life.* Eyre & Spottiswoode 1965.
RAEBURN, ANTONIA. *The Militant Suffragettes.* Michael Joseph 1973.
RAY, JOHN. *A History of Britain, 1900-1939.* Pergamon Press 1967.
READ, DONALD. *Documents from Edwardian England.* Harrap 1973.
READ, DONALD. *Edwardian England, 1901-1915: Society and Politics.* Harrap 1972.
READE, L. *Marconi and the Discovery of Wireless.* Faber 1963.
ROWLAND, JOHN. *The Automobile Man: The Story of Henry Ford.* Lutterworth Press 1973.
THOMAS, DAVID ST JOHN. *The Motor Revolution.* Longman 1961.

Acknowledgements

We wish to thank the following individuals and organizations for their assistance and for making available material in their collections.

Key to picture positions:
(T) top; (C) centre; (L) left; (B) bottom; (R) right and combinations; for example (TC) top centre.

Ally Sloper's Half-Holiday p. 7(TL), 50(C)
Archiv Gerstenberg p. 44(BL)
Archivo Casaola p. 51(R)
Batchelor, John p. 15(B), 39(T)
Belgrade Military Museum p. 49(B), 55(TL)
Bertarelli Collection p. 9(BR)
Bettman Archive p. 13(BR), 18(TL), 53(L)
Bibby's Annual p. 34(T)
Biblioteque Nationale, Paris p. 37(B), 43(T), 57(TR)
Binney, Marcus p. 41(TR)
Bradford City Library p. 27(TR)
British Museum p. 29(BL)
Brown Brothers p. 38(L)
Culver Pix p. 10(BR), 18(BR)
Deutsches Museum, Munich p. 53(CL)
Dr Ricardo Jucker Collection p. 40(BL)
Editions Rencontre p. 3
Editions Sociales, Paris p. 36(BR)
Elegante Welt, Taslemka p. 2
Eric Lessing-Magnum, Paris p. 8-9
Ernst Freud p. 53(CR)
Ferrers Gallery p. 21(BL)
Foto Krupp, Essen p. 44(BR)
Gernsheim Collection p. 16(TL), 38(R)
Gilbert, Martin p. 26(T)
GLC Photo Library p. 17(TL)
Government Archives, Pretoria p. 25(TL)
Harlingue Violet p. 55(TR)
Hulton Picture Library p. 4(L), 4(R), 5(TR), 8(TL), 12(BL), 13(TR), 18(BL), 22(T), 27(TL), 36(BC)

Jacques Doucet Collection p. 40-41
Kaiser Wilhelm Museum, Krefeld p. 16(BL)
Kenneth Griffith Collection p. 50(T)
Keystone Press p. 53(BL)
Kodak Museum p. 12(BR)
Kyodo News Service, Tokyo p. 30(BL), 52(R)
L'Assiette au Beurre p. 25(TR)
La Vie Parisienne p. 9(TR)
Leipzige Illustrierte p. 8(BL)
Le Petit Journal Illustre p. 31(TR), 36(TL), 36(BL)
Library of Congress p. 5(TL), 5(BR), 13(BL), 17(TR), 17(BR), 19(B), 21(BR)
Life p. 14(BL)
L'Illustration p. 17(BL), 55(B)
London Museum p. 10(TL)
London Transport Board p. 14(TL)
Macdonald Educational Visual Books "Cars" p. 14(BR)
Mander and Mitchenson p. 56(BR)
Mansell Collection p. 16(BR), 20(B), 31(B), 32(TL), 37(TL), 52(L)
Mary Evans Picture Library p. 15(TL)
Musee des Arts Decoratifs, Paris p. 6(L)
Musee des Beaux Arts, Rouen p. 7(TR)
Museo d'Arte Moderna, Milan p. 35
Museum of Modern Art, New York p. 40(TL)
National Army Museum, Camberley p. 54(T)
National Army Museum, Sandhurst p. 24-5, 27(BL), 27(BR)
National Maritime Museum, Greenwich p. 42-3
Novosti p. 31(CL), 32(BR), 33(BL), 50(B), 56(BL), 57(TL)
Oscar Telegram p. 45(BL)
Paul Popper Limited p. 29(BR), 33(BR)
Piancastelli Forlil p. 53(BR)
Punch p. 54(B)
Royal Court Theatre p. 56(TL)
Science Museum, London p. 12(TL)

Snark p. 7(BL), 30(BR)
Sport and General p. 11(TL)
Städtische Museen, Vienna p. 5(BL)
Tate Gallery p. 41(BR)
Thomas Mann Archiv, Zurich p. 57(TC)
Ullstein p. 13(TL), 23(BL), 44(TL)
Victoria and Albert Museum p. 20(T)
Viollet, Roger p. 6(R), 9(TL), 13(TC)
Walker Art Gallery, Liverpool p. 22(B)

Editor
Tim Healey

Assistant Editor
Susan Ward

Projects
Maurice Clifton

Cover picture: Advertisement for a French car.

Back cover: *Vole Wright!* (Fly Wright), a French cartoon satirizing aviation.

Note: in this book, all foreign words, titles of books, films etc. are in *italics* e.g. *The Doctor's Dilemma.*

If we have unwittingly infringed any copyright in any picture or photograph reproduced in this publication we tender our sincere apologies and will be glad of the opportunity, upon being satisfied as to the owner's title, to pay an appropriate fee as if we had been able to obtain prior permission.